& The Comfort Foods that Keep Them Going

The Thin Gold Line honors all those who serve in public safety telecommunications, including police dispatchers, fire dispatchers, and ambulance dispatchers. The Thin Gold Line can also represent Security Guards, Loss Prevention Associates, and Search and Rescue Personnel.

Copyright 2021© by Steve & Missy Haston | From Capes to Aprons

All rights reserved. No part of this publication may be reproduced, stored in a retrieval system or transmitted in any form or by any means electronic, mechanical, photocopying recording or otherwise without the prior written permission of the publisher.

First edition November 2021

Logo, Cover and Interior Design by Regina Rexrode | Point n' Click Publishing
Stock Photos courtesy of AdobeStock.com and Shutterstock
ISBN (paperback): 9798985159103
ISBN (epub) 9798985159110

Published by From Capes to Aprons, LLC

Dedicated to all fellow dispatchers who have worked and continue to work in this job. We have worked 12 hour shifts, weekends, nights, zero dark thirty hours. We have missed Christmas and other holidays and special days with our families. We are the first person you never will see or hear about on the scene. We are the ears until our fellow emergency responders arrive on the scene. We hear things we never want to hear. The field first responders see things they can never forget. We are there for you day and night, 24 hours a day, 7 days a week.

~Missy Birnell Haston~

CONTENTS

INTRODUCTION 1
UNDERSTANDING DISPATCH 2
DISPATCH TERMINOLOGY 3
POLICE CODES 5

MISSY

Dispatcher Bio 7
10-56 Beef 9
    Hard to Hear 9
Cheese Ball 12
Chocolate Eclair Cake 12
    Delivered Three Babies 13
Chicken and Rice Casserole 14
    Domestic Abuse 15
    Incredible Denial 16
    WARM and Fuzzy 17
Meatball and Sausage Nibblers 17
    Monkey 18
Hot German Potato Salad 19
Chicken Velvet Soup 19
    Translator 20
    Horse 21
homemade Guacamole 21
    Quicksand 22
    Suicides 23
Salsa Meatloaf 24
    Hauling ASS 24
Crunchy Tuna Casserole 25
Dispatcher Bio 27

CINDY

Dispatcher Bio 27
Banana Bread 28
    Pat Down 29
    Cardboard Cutout 29
    Sparing Dummy 29
Camping Pumpkin Pie 30
    Miscarriage 30
    Someone Stole My Spice 31
Healthy Zucchini Bread 31

BECKY

Dispatcher Bio 33
Cake Balls 34
    Shots Fired 35
    Dispatcher of the Year Award 36
    My Dispatch Family 38
Macaroni & Cheese 39

911 Emergency Dispatchers, Public Safety Responders | i

Chicken Fiesta Soup	39
Escape	40
Child in Danger	41
Baby Locked in Car	42
Chocolate Chip Cookies	43
Lifesaver Award	45
Fishbowl Guy	46
Crock Pot Chicken Noodle Soup	47
Chocolate & Peanut Butter Ritz Cookies	47
I Got That	48
Attempted Suicide	49

LISA

Dispatcher Bio	51
Lisa's Powder Sugar Cookies	52
Multi-Car Pile Up	53
Fudge	54
Training Classes	54
Old Fashioned Biscuits	55
Angry Geese	55
Civil War	56
Bacon Cauliflower Salad	56
Insta Pot Salsa Chicken	57
Peel Away the Pounds Soup	57
Contemplating Suicide	58
Sweet Potato Souffle	59
Back Yard Deer	59
They Know Me	60
Lisa Lisa	61

PAM

Dispatcher Bio	63
Teesh's Cucumber Dip	64
Pork Steak & Potatoes	65
Kidnapped	65
Southern Green Beans	66
Smothered Meat	66
Dispatch shenanigans	67
Shorts	68
After School Cookies	69
Dayna's Wacky Cake	69
Girl	70
Cornbread Dressing	70
Pig	71
Ham 'n Beans	71
How Dead is He?	72
Cream Pie	72
Goulash	73
Pasta Salad	73
Sweet Potatoes	74
Fried Corn	74
Ride a Longs	75

BOB

Police Officer Bio 77
   Flipped me the bird 78
   Impaired Drivers 78
   Ball Python 79
   Appliance Store 79
   See My Brother 80
   We Both Scream 80
   Breaking Into Cars 81
   Syphon Gas 81

STEVE

FireFighter Bio 83
Family Roast 84
   Two Missing Three Year Olds 85
   Apartment Arson Fire 86
   Young and Dumb 87
Mac-N-Cheese 88
   Breech Birth 89
Dirty Rice and Shrimp 90
   Fish Tank Feed 90
Fire House Chili 91
   He Walks on Water 92
Crispy Skin Salmon 93
Croque Monsieur Part 1 - Bechamel 94
Croque Monsieur Part 2 - Sandwich 95
Chicken Noodle Soup 96
   Fish Tank Smack Down 97
Grilled Pork Chop 98
   Pez Finger 98
Purple Potato Mash 99
   What's that Smell? 100
   Man on the Run 102

911 Emergency Dispatchers, Public Safety Responders | iii

INTRODUCTION

Communications centers across the country operate 24 hours a day, seven days a week, with no exceptions every year. The dispatchers stand ready to receive calls from citizens, visitors, and anyone needing some form of assistance. Whether it's for simple information or a life-threatening traumatic emergency situation.

Dispatchers in Hamilton County Indiana are highly trained professionals who operate complex 800-megahertz radio technology systems, allowing them to maintain critical communications with every emergency responder in the county and surrounding counties. They are trained to navigate multiple layers of complicated Computer Aided Dispatch software (CAD). Dispatchers are also masters of multitasking; they must answer the 9-1-1 emergency calls, collect harrowing information, control the conversation, enter the information in the CAD, announce the information over the radio to the responders, provide lifesaving instructions to the caller, continue to communicate updates with the responders while they are en route, and so much more simultaneously. Our Hamilton County dispatchers, depending on the call they are answering, must be counselors, educators, doctors, lawyers, zoologists, moms, map navigators, and more. Just try to imagine any type of call, and they have probably taken it.

As you can imagine, dispatching is labeled as one of the highest stress careers in the United States. In most cases, dispatchers are the true first, first responders for a disaster or emergency, before any other responders arrive on scene. Exposures to these all too often disturbing calls can lead a dispatcher to illness, psychological problems, post-traumatic stress, or to just get burnt out. There are many ways to cope with these high levels of stress, and dispatchers receive training and counseling on these topics. Many agencies also have programs in place to help and support the dispatcher. Most importantly, dispatchers take care of each other and become highly skilled at recognizing when their co-workers are struggling and how to comfort and support them.

One thing all dispatchers have in common, as we all do, is their love of food. A good meal can, most of the time, cut through the stress of the job and life. From Capes to Aprons: 9-1-1 Dispatchers and Their Amazing Stories is a cookbook like no other. More than just excellent recipes, it includes amazing stories from real Hamilton County dispatchers. The creator of this book, Missy, was a career dispatcher for over 23 years and was inspired by her many experiences to create a unique collection of recipes and stories.

Missy and our contributing authors were a tight-knit group of dispatchers who handled hundreds of harrowing emergency calls and many hilarious ones too. All of our authors also found comfort in cooking as a way to decompress after certain calls or a stressful day.

From Capes to Aprons: 911 Dispatchers and Their Amazing Stories is the culmination of the meals that have been created and inspired by our dispatchers. Hamilton County is fortunate to have these dedicated professionals standing guard and ready to serve the community every hour of every day. Our Hamilton County dispatchers deserve our respect and gratitude because they save lives, help people, and sacrificially serve the community. We hope you will enjoy the recipes and stories from their many years of combined service!

UNDERSTANDING DISPATCH

Have you ever wondered how the 9-1-1 emergency dispatch calls really work?

Let's dive right into it.

Unfortunately, someone is having a bad day. Something is about to happen that is going to require this person to seek help beyond what they can provide to themselves. It could be something minor, like a tree branch across the road. It could be something ridiculous like someone calling because a dog is barking in the middle of the day. It could be something more serious like a theft, or a catastrophic event such as a cardiac arrest. No matter the type of call, 9-1-1 dispatchers are ready to provide directions to life saving instructions. So how does it all fall in place?

Well let's say that unfortunate event just happened. It is a cardiac arrest at a workplace. We will use the name Harvey. Harvey starts complaining of bad chest pains and tells his co-workers he is having a heart attack. Harvey is told to sit down and they will call 9-1-1. As the co-worker is getting their phone Harvey collapses.

Every minute counts, time is of the essence to save Harvey's life.

9-1-1 is dialed. Through the marvel of technology, the call whether from a landline or cell phone, is routed to the 9-1-1 call center known as a Public Safety Answering Point (PSAP), in Hamilton County this is a secure facility. In the 9-1-1 call center there are multiple stations set up. Each station has six computer monitors; a phone monitor, three CAD monitor, one monitor for a map, and one for the radio with several radio channels. The dispatcher is a master of multi-tasking as they must continually scan all of these monitors, especially when the call is received. Each of these screens display different information that is vital to get the emergency handled in the most efficient and timely manner possible. This is often easier said than done. The caller is almost always panicked, and that causes delays in the transfer of information.

The incoming calls are routed to the station and answered by the Call Taker, the dispatcher taking the initial call for assistance. Immediately displayed on one of the monitors is information about the call, such as their caller ID. Another monitor has a map that loads the caller's location if it is available. When the call taker first answers the incoming call they will use the phrase "9-1-1 what is the location of your emergency?" At this point the composure of the person making the call has a lot to do with how expeditiously the call taker can get help responding. As soon as the caller identifies the nature of the emergency, known as the "Call Type", the call taker enters it into the CAD. This automatically opens a series of predetermined questions based on the call type. In our case the questions are focused on cardiac arrest. It is also important to note here that additional information is simultaneously updating on all of the monitors. Information like the predetermined apparatus for this call type, mapping, jurisdiction, etc. Now as you can imagine these predetermined questions are medical in nature such as are they breathing, are they turning blue around the lips, age, height and weight, have they been sick, etc. The CAD uses what is known as conditional logic, so based on how the questions are answered the next questions are generated. If everything we just described went smoothly, from the moment the 9-1-1 call was received to this next step only about 20 seconds have passed. If however; the caller was panicked or uncooperative the next step may have been delayed up to 60 seconds. This is a lot of lost time when trying to save lives. The call then goes to the dispatch screen. In this case Fire Dispatch. The Fire Dispatcher tones out the correct apparatus in the recommended jurisdiction and then will hit the accept button in the CAD to attach the apparatus to the call. and hits the "accept" button that puts the apparatus on the call. The firefighters and paramedics can see what has been typed into the and will be prepared for what they are about to arrive on. Notes like, CPR started, Nitro given are phrases they can see and help them plan for what they will do on arrival. They, like dispatch, have a map on their in truck computers to to map the quickest route to the call. Once medical help has arrived dispatch will continue to update notes in the CAD given by medical personnel on scene to track events and times of the call for report taking.

Rich or poor it doesn't matter. People are people. Some of them need constant attention in the form of 9-1-1 assistance, others, even at age 60, 70, 80, or even 90, have never called 9-1-1. How do we explain this?

Dispatch Terminology

CODE	TERM
Ten / Signal Codes:	Numerals used in place of words to describe an occurrence or situation. (ex....10-4 (acknowledgment) and Signal 27 (traffic stop).
District/Beat:	An area for the day that an office patrols.
Driving Complaint:	Someone driving in a manner that the complainant deems dangerous.
Dispatcher:	Highly trained person who for all intents and purposes is the first, first responders.
Dedicated Channels:	Each municipality has their own radio channel to communicate with dispatch.
Headquarters:	Console/desk where stolen items, missing people, wanted subjects are entered into the national database.
Supervisor	Console- One who can oversee the events of the room and capabilities to help out with anything.
Call Takers:	A console that is dedicated to answer non-emergency and emergency calls.
CAD:	Computer Aided Dispatch System- a computerized database that allows us to track units and create and maintain a history of calls.
Pat Down:	Where an officer or jail employee feels over the clothing of a suspect to see if they have any weapons or drugs on them.
Run Times:	These are the timestamps for every incident from start to finish.
EMS:	Emergency Medical Services
ALS:	Advanced Life Support
BLS:	Basic Life Support
mic clicked:	Pushing the button on the radio as if to say something, but nothing was said. Is usually a quick way for someone to say OK or I understand without actually speaking.
Car to Car:	Is a channel where police officers can talk to each other without taking up radio time on the main channel.
ANI:	Automatic Number Identifier: Displays the 9-1-1 callers phone number on the phone screen prior to answering.
ALI:	Automatic Location Identifier: Displays the 9-1-1 callers phone number, location, and name.
ATL:	Attempt to locate.
BOLO:	Be on the lookout (used in teletypes)
Calls for Service:	Calls received by dispatch for patrol / ems units to respond.
FTO:	Field training officer.
GOA:	Gone on arrival.

CODE	TERM
DL or 10-27:	drivers license.
10-28:	vehicle plate.
Vin:	Vehicle Identification number.
RMS:	Record management system: Computerized database that contains the names, DOB, and other personal information that has previously been gathered on someone.
DWI:	Driving while intoxicated.
DWS:	Driving while suspended.
FTA:	Failure to appear.
HazMat:	hazardous material that could represent a danger to someone.
Incident Number:	a number that is created when a call is entered into the CASD.
MDT:	Mobile data terminal (in car computer)
Mutual Aid:	an agreement between cities to help each other out when additional equipment or personnel is needed.
NCIC :	National Crime Information Center. Checking or entering something wanted or stolen. Maintained and owned by the FBI
NLETS:	National Law Enforcement Telecommunications System:
ORI:	a unique 9 digit combination of letters and numbers that is used to identify an agencies NLETS terminal.
PO:	Protective order.
SOP:	Standard Operating Procedure.
SWAT:	Special Weapons and Tactics.
TDD:	Telecommunications device for the deaf.
Traffic Hazard:	Any object in the roadway that may present a danger to motorists.
ETOH:	Intoxicated subject.
TX:	Phone

Capes to Aprons • Stories and Recipes

Police 10 Codes

Code	Meaning	Code	Meaning	Code	Meaning
10-1	Unable to Copy - Change Location	10-35	Major Crime Alert	10-69	Message Received
10-2	Signal Good	10-36	Correct Time	10-70	Fire Alarm
10-3	Stop Transmitting	10-37	(Investigate) Suspicious Vehicle	10-71	Advise Nature of Fire
10-4	Acknoledgement (OK)	10-38	Stopping Suspicious Vehicle	10-72	Report progress on Fire
10-5	Relay	10-39	Urgent-Use Light, Siren	10-73	Smoke Report
10-6	Busy-Unless Urgent	10-40	Silent Run-No Light, Siren	10-74	Negative
10-7	Out of Service	10-41	Beginning Tour of Duty	10-75	In Contact with ___
10-8	In Service	10-42	Ending Tour of Duty	10-76	En Route ___
10-9	Repeat	10-43	Information	10-77	ETA (Estimamated Time of Arrival)
10-10	Fight in Progress	10-44	Permission to Leave ___ for ___	10-78	Need Assistance
10-11	Dog Case	10-45	Animal Carcass at ___	10-79	Notify Coroner
10-12	Stand By (Stop)	10-46	Assist Motorist	10-80	Chase in Progress
10-13	Weather - Road Report	10-47	Emergency Road Repair at___	10-81	Breatherlizer Report
10-14	Prowler Report	10-48	Traffic Standard Repair at ___	10-82	Reserve Lodging
10-15	Civil Disturbance	10-49	Traffic Light Out at ___	10-83	Work School Crossing at ___
10-16	Domestic Problem	10-50	Accident (F, PI, PD)[1]	10-84	If Meeting ___ Advise ETA
10-17	Meet Complainant	10-51	Wrecker Needed	10-85	Delay Due to
10-18	Quickly	10-52	Ambulance Needed	10-86	Officer / Operator on Duty
10-19	Return to___	10-53	Road Blocked at ___	10-87	Pickup / Distribute Checks
10-20	Location	10-54	Livestock on Highway	10-88	Present Telephone # of ___
10-21	Call (___) by Phone	10-55	Intoxicated Driver	10-89	Bomb Threat
10-22	Disregard	10-56	INtoxicated Pedestrian	10-90	Bank Alarm at ___
10-23	Arrived at Scene	10-57	Hit and Run (F, PI, PD)[1]	10-91	Pick Up Prisoner / Subjet
10-24	Assignment Completed	10-58	Direct Traffic	10-92	Improperly Parked Vehicle
10-25	Report in Person (Meet)	10-59	Convoy or Escort	10-93	Blockade
10-26	Detaining Subject, Expedite	10-60	Squad in Vicinity	10-94	Drag Racing
10-27	(Driver) License Information	10-61	Personnel in Area	10-95	Prisoner / Subject in Custody
10-28	Vehicle Registration Information	10-62	Reply to Message	10-96	Mental Subject
10-29	Check for Wanted	10-63	Prepare Make Written Copy	10-97	Check (Test) Signal
10-30	Unnecessary Use of Radio	10-64	Message for Local Delivery	10-98	Prison / Jail Break
10-31	Crime in Progress	10-65	Net Message Assignment	10-99	Wanted / Stolen Indicated
10-32	Man with Gun	10-66	Message Cancellation	10-101	Waht is Status?
10-33	Emergency	10-67	Clear for Net Message	10-106	Status is secure
10-34	Riot	10-68	Dispatch Information		**(1) F - Fire, PI - Personal Injury, PD - Property Damage**

Reference: Radar Information Center - CopRadar.com

DISPATCHER BIO

Missy Birnell Haston. I was born Melissa Jenee' Birnell (Missy) in Logansport, Indiana, on September 15, 1965, to Jean Ann (nee Layman) Birnell and Larry Jim Birnell, a Marine veteran of the Cuban Missile Crisis. I was raised in the small town of Walton, Indiana, population about 1,000, just 12 miles away. It was there in Walton, where most of my family lived, that I developed my mischievous and humorous side. I was an only child and the baby of the family for a long time, so I became little Miss Princess. In other words, I was spoiled. I had my dad wrapped around my finger. Sure, he would take me fishing, make me help him in the garage, and ride mini bikes, but after whining and pouty lips, he always gave in to what I wanted. I had dogs, a deer, my own TV, a stereo system with huge speakers, and new bikes. My mom was a bit upset about the stereo system because it was very loud and better than her old one. Since my dad was the volunteer fire chief for years, all the firemen also spoiled me. I got to play ping pong on Sundays with them. And my dad would use the town equipment to plow the snow in a circle in our large yard, then add a large roll of plastic and fill it with water from a fire truck to make an ice-skating rink, open to all the kids. The spoil list went on and on!

Then at age 13, tragedy struck, and my dad passed away unexpectedly. This was a terrible time for my mom and me. Thankfully, we had lots of family support to help us through the next couple of years. I didn't think I could make it through high school without my dad. My mom was wonderful, but being widowed at 34 was so hard on her, and she had to get a job in a factory to make ends meet. I never knew back then how bad it was for her, until I got older. But most of my teachers in my small town knew what I had gone through, and they helped me more than they will ever know. My best friend was Tina Plank. I practically lived at her house, and her mom was my second mom, she was always there if my mom wasn't available. After we graduated from Lewis Cass High School, Tina went to Indiana State University, and I chose an easier route at Professional Careers Institute.

At PCI, I studied medical and dental office administration, and when school was finished, I had to intern at a doctor's or dentist's office. I was assigned to Northside Cardiology at St Vincent Hospital in Indianapolis. They hired me after my internship, and I worked there for two years - until I started taking karate lessons and married the instructor. After we had our first son, I stayed home for two years to care for him. I got very bored, so I got a front desk job at a dental office. After that, I was offered a job as a listing secretary at a real estate company that would let me work around my son's school schedule. I would just leave work and get him and bring him back to work with me if there was still work to be done. My husband was a firefighter, so on the days he worked 24 hours, I was full-time mom. My son loved going to the office with me, especially because he liked to torture the high school girls who answered the phones after school. I got pregnant with my second son while at this real estate company, nine years after my first son was born. I was told I couldn't get pregnant again, but miracles do happen. My second son was born with asthma and breathing problems because I was toxemic during this pregnancy. I had to leave my beloved job and stay home for two years until his lungs developed.

At that time, my husband encouraged me to apply for an opening at the Hamilton County Sheriff's Department as a part-time dispatcher. It worked for a while because I would only go in to train on the nights he was home from the fire department. But shortly after being hired, a full-time spot opened, and I was asked to take it. I was worried about leaving my 18-month-old baby with asthma, but a friend of mine from the real estate office had opened up her own daycare. So, I took the full-time position. It was on the second shift, which was from 2 p.m. to 10 p.m. I started training, and it didn't take long before I thought everyone there was nuts! My trainer would hit me with a ruler if I messed up and then laugh. She even went through my purse when I took a break, and that's when I learned that if you can't beat 'em, join 'em. So I went through her things, called her by her last name as she did me, and learned to block the ruler. It really was all in good fun. It's easy to get depressed in the atmosphere of a 911 dispatch center, so humor and shenanigans were our coping mechanisms.

I worked the second shift for five years, and those hours were hard with a family. Then I spent four years on third shift (10 p.m. to 6.a.m.), and that was even harder with a family. Finally, I got enough seniority to go to day shift (6 a.m. to 2 p.m.). But changes came to the shift hours because many staff were not happy with the weekend scheduling. It had never bothered me because my husband also worked a rotating schedule and worked weekends and holidays, just like me. And my mom was always available to take care of my kids when we both ended up working on the same weekend. Eventually, after several experimental shift schedules, they settled on 12-hour shifts: 5 a.m. to 5 p.m. and 5 p.m. to 5 a.m. I was lucky I got the day shift. Even still, twelve hours of being plugged into a console with constant talking in an earpiece from either a phone call or an officer or firefighters was exhausting. When the COVID-19 pandemic hit, I retired, after 23 years. I just could not wear a mask for twelve hours a day. I still applaud all my co-workers who made it through that time.

I look back on my career as a dispatcher, and I think of all the calls I took. I have delivered babies, talked people out of suicide, heard people take their last breath, given CPR instructions thousands of times, and talked to children who walked in from school and found a parent who had committed suicide. Most people do not think about or understand how heart-wrenching these calls can be - or how hard it is to often not know how an emergency situation ended. You want to just run out of the room, but you have to keep that child or caller safe until help arrives.

I have talked to a mom who found her 3-year-old son's shoes by a pond because she turned her back for a second. She couldn't swim, and I couldn't let her go in the pond. We didn't know for sure if he was in there. But the divers came, and he was. I can still hear her sobs and heartbreak. I was crying right along with her. I will never know if she is alright, but I think of her now and again.

I think about a teenage boy who was with a friend when a car full of other teens picked them up and beat them up badly because the friend had been dating a girl who another boy liked. I took the call from the one boy who survived, though injured, and managed to call 911. He couldn't tell me exactly where his friend was but said the friend was in very bad shape and covered in blood. After I gently told him to go outside and go with the officers to show them where his friend was, he asked if he could just talk to me and never hang up. I knew he was in shock, but I had to get help for his friend. He found his way to his friend with the officers and medics. The friend was beaten so badly that he was mentally damaged for the rest of his life. I think about those boys.

I think about the mom who fell asleep while nursing her baby, and the baby suffocated. The school shooting. I think of everyone with whom I have had to share the most horrific time of their life on a 911 call. I'm glad I was there to help. But they still haunt my dreams. I wish I could somehow know if I mattered, or if they remember it as much as I do. It really does take a toll on your mind and body - the stress, the long hours, the new protocols that seem to come out every day which you can't possibly keep up with, the cringe if you have to ask a question out of order while knowing that those who listen will mark off points from your score sheet they keep. But I loved this job.

Although the new protocols made me realize it was time for me to go, I wouldn't trade the old days for anything. I made lifelong friends in dispatch. Some of them are closer to me than my own family. We often worked together more than we were at home. Though there were many bad times and calls, we got through them together and could usually get each other to smile or laugh just to get through the day. We leaned on each other. And no amount of counseling could replace that…..ever.

10-56 BEEF

by Missy

Prep Time: 30 wn. | Cook Time: Aprox. 1 hr

INGREDIENTS

- 2 Tbps. Butter
- 2 lbs. Stew Beef (cubed)
- 1 (6 oz.) can Tomato Paste
- 1 tsp. Minced Garlic
- 1 tsp. Thyme
- 1 Bay Leaf
- ½ tsp. Paprika
- 2 lg. onions (chopped)
- 2 c. Beef Broth
- 1 c. Dry Red Wine (Pino Noir)
- 1 c. Flour to cover the beef
- Rice or Egg Noodles (cooked as directed on package)

INSTRUCTIONS:

1. Dredge the stew meat into the flour until coated.
2. On the stovetop, cook the cubed floured beef in a large pot like a dutch oven in the butter until browned about 5 minutes
3. Add all the remaining ingredients and cook on medium low until the beef is tender for about and hour and a half. Stir and check often
4. Salt and pepper to taste
5. Serve over rice or egg noodles

HINTS: use extra wine, hence 10-56 beef. 10-56 means intoxicated person, I also cook my rice or noodles in beef broth just to give it extra flavor.

HARD TO HEAR

by Missy

One evening on second shift in the dispatch center, we had a fatality on a major interstate through our county. My coworker was on a call from a girl who was going northbound in the southbound lanes, trying to get her to safely pull off the road, when the girl's vehicle was struck head on. She and the other vehicle occupants were killed instantly. It was a tragic accident. The girl was not from around here and was young and didn't know how to correct her mistake. Of course, all of us poured our dispatch love on that call taker. It's never a good thing in our profession to hear someone's last words, and knowing she was terrified made it even worse.

The interstate was shut down. The sheriff and coroner were called. The crash team was called out. They investigate fatalities by taking measurements and rates of speed to see who was at fault. Unfortunately for this poor girl's family it was her fault, just from turning the wrong way. It was dark at night, and it's a mistake made more often than people would believe.

The calls that involved me that night were some that rank with the best "How stupid can you be?" calls. A female called and asked if she could just go around the blockades because she had stuff to do. No time to wait in traffic! The first few times she called, I tried to be as polite as I could be: "Ma'am there is a serious accident and the road is shut down for investigation and getting patient care." She would hang up and call right back! I became

continues...

familiar with her cell phone number, so I told my coworkers to let me answer every time she called. She kept hoping for someone else. We played this game several times before she asked for my supervisor. I am not and never was a supervisor, but I was the one on duty with the most seniority that night so I said, "I am the supervisor." Another hang up and then another call. This time she wanted me to pull an officer from the scene to come and talk to her. So I played along and asked her what kind of car she was in and where she was. She told me that she drove a white Cadillac and where she was, then indicated that her car "stood out, it wouldn't be hard to find." I typed all of this in the CAD (Computer Aided Dispatch), along with her name and phone number.

I then contacted the police in command of the scene and asked him to call in at his convenience. When he called, I explained to him this constant caller and that she had told me she would keep calling until she was helped out of the traffic. He was instantly furious. He asked for the vehicle description and advised me to type it all in the CAD. He told me to call her back and tell her that the lieutenant said the family of the victims appreciates her patience. Usually we do not say words like "fatality" to a general caller, but he gave me permission. So a tad happy that I got to yell at her and not face repercussions, I called the woman and told her that I spoke with a lieutenant on her behalf and that he has her name, number, and vehicle description.

"Good!" she said.

" BUT!" I continued, "He said to tell you that you are no better than anyone else waiting in traffic, nor are you the only one inconvenienced. He also said to tell you he was sure the families of the victims appreciated her patience and that she should hope and pray it wasn't anyone she knew."

She started sputtering, but I cut her off and continued:

"AFTER the poor victims are finally extricated from their mangled vehicles and the road closure released, all the officers on the scene will be looking for your 'stand out white caddy' to have a chat with you for harassing 911 dispatchers while knowing that they were busy working a fatal scene."

I went on to explain every single detail that goes into tragedies like this. She was silent. I thought she had hung up. Then she quickly said, "Thank you" and disconnected. It's sad that telling her off made me feel good. At least for a few minutes, until my next caller.

A male stuck in the same traffic backup called 911 demanding an escort. His girlfriend was bleeding all over his seats. I immediately thought of miscarriage or child birth.

"Is your girlfriend pregnant? I asked.

"No!" he replied, in a very condescending tone.

"Well is she hemorrhaging from an operation, then?" I said.

"No!" he yelled at me. "She just started her period."

I was stunned into silence. I gathered myself and asked why he would need an escort for a woman on her period. He advised that she was staining his seats! He just wanted to get to a gas station to clean his car! With my newfound freedom to talk bluntly to stupid callers, I laid into him. I asked him if he realized that people had lost their lives and there was still debris all over the road and that the officers could care less about his girlfriend's period and there being blood on his car seat. He started to yell back. So I told him that if he called back I would proceed as with my previous constant caller, and would he like me to add his vehicle, name and phone number to my growing list? He said no and never called back.

Hell hath no fury like a dispatcher trying to protect her officers and EMS personnel on the scene of a tragedy. I know that what they are seeing there hurts them. I know that they only care about the scene and the safety of everyone involved. They have a job to do. If you happen to be one that would actually call 911 just because you were stuck in traffic because of an accident, ask yourself, "What if that was my family or friend? How will their families cope? What if the officers and firefighters dragging out the mangled bodies were my husband or father or friend?" Be thankful that you are just stuck in traffic for awhile and you get to go home. You do not have bad images in your head. You won't have nightmares about making a notification to the victim's families and seeing them fall apart at the news you just delivered. Be grateful it's not a funeral you will not have to attend. You will not eventually develop PTSD from the thousands of scenes like this that happen every year. Maybe instead, think about how, if you had been just a little faster or had started out sooner, this could have been you. But most of all, know this: we - the dispatchers, firefighters, police officers, paramedics, and EMTs - will always be there for your emergency if it ever happens, and we will deflect calls like these in order to help you in your time of need.

Missy Birnell Haston on a ride along with an officer for training purposes. I got to hold the radar gun! We get 2 ride alongs with police and 2 ride alongs with fire per year.

CHEESE BALL

by Missy

I like to put it under a cheese dome....you can also roll in nuts to make it look prettier!

Prep Time: **15 min.**

INGREDIENTS

2 pkgs. Dried Beef
1 bunch Green Onions
2 (8 oz.) boxes of Cream Cheese
Assorted Crackers

INSTRUCTIONS:

1. Chop up the dried beef and the green onions
2. Mix together with the cream cheese
3. Form into a ball and serve with cheese and crackers.

CHOCOLATE ECLAIR CAKE

by Missy

INGREDIENTS

2 (5 oz.) boxes White Chocolate Instant Pudding
1 box Graham Crackers
3 ½ c. Milk
1 (8 oz.) tub Cool Whip
2 (16 oz.) cans Milk Chocolate Frosting

INSTRUCTIONS:

1. Beat pudding and the milk with an electric mixer until thick.
2. Fold in Cool Whip (thawed)
3. Layer a 9 x 13" pan starting with the graham crackers.
4. Pour half the pudding mixture on top, then add another layer of graham crackers and rest of pudding on top of that.
5. Add the final layer of graham crackers.
6. Frost with the top with the Milk Chocolate Frosting
7. (I melt the frosting or a few seconds in the microwave while still in the open can so it can pour on and using 2 cans makes it thicker)
8. Refrigerate over night and the frosting has the consistency of ganache!

Delicious!

DELIVERED THREE BABIES

by Missy

I have helped deliver three babies over the phone during my career as a dispatcher. The first started as a call from a frantic female stating that she heard crying from her daughter's bedroom, and when she entered the room there was a newborn baby on the floor. Completely shocked, she kept repeating over the phone, "Why is there a baby here?" I knew that we had to attend to the baby right away, so I told her to wrap it in a warm towel or blanket and check the umbilical cord. She stated that the cord looked like it had been cut with bloody scissors that were on the floor by the baby. The baby was at serious risk of bleeding out, so I told her to get a shoelace and tie it around the cord, snugly but not too tight, about four inches from the baby's body. Once she had gotten the baby warm and tied off the cord, I asked where her daughter was. After searching she found her in the shower. Following protocol, I instructed the mother to get her out of the shower and lay her down on the floor until the medics arrived, which they did shortly.

A bit later, one of the medics called in for his run times and asked me, "Who had the caller tie the shoestring on the umbilical cord?"

I swallowed hard, thinking I had done something wrong, and answered "Me."

"Well you saved that baby's life," he told me. "It was going to bleed out."

I got tears in my eyes. When he asked how I knew what to tell them to do, I told him about the cards we had that walked us step by step through almost any situation (this was back in the "old days"), and he was impressed.

I am so happy that I was able to help keep that brand new baby alive. And I still wonder how the mother didn't know that her daughter was pregnant.

My second and favorite delivery was a husband who had his pregnant wife in the bathroom on a toilet and called us to say that she was in labor. I told him right away to get her off the toilet and lying down on the floor ("Face up," I told him, because sometimes people actually ask if the pregnant woman should lay on her stomach, believe it or not!). As she got on the floor, everything below the waist removed, I kept hearing a child saying, "Why is mommy on the floor? Mommy, can you brush my hair?" The woman giving birth was so kind to her child and just said, "Mommy is a little busy right now, sweetheart." I was amazed at her composure! The child kept talking throughout the entire delivery while the father, panicked but steady, followed my instructions.

When the baby was born, just before medics arrived, I said, "Congratulations! Is it a boy or girl?" He sobbed and just said, "I don't know," as the medics took over.

My final over-the-phone delivery was a male who called to say his wife was in labor and he was lost and needed directions to the hospital. When I asked him to tell me where he was, he didn't know. After I prompted him to look for a road sign and he finally found one, I put the location in the CAD, only to discover that he was lost in the middle of a huge subdivision. I could hear the female screaming in the background, "The baby is coming now!" I started medics to his location as I told him to pull over. But he did not want to pull over and kept driving. I said "Sir, your wife said she can feel the baby coming, and you are not close to the hospital. I've started an ambulance, and I want you to pull over right now and update me on the street you are on!" He argued back, so I had to verbally slap him by saying, "YOU HAVE TO PULL OVER! GET YOUR WIFE IN THE BACKSEAT AND REMOVE HER CLOTHING FROM THE WAIST DOWN NOW!" He finally obeyed and as soon as he removed her pants the baby started coming. The ambulance arrived just in time to catch it.

One of the challenging things about being a dispatcher is that we often have to weigh the pros and cons of a situation in a matter of seconds. In this case I based my decision on the female's screams I could hear in the background. I also had to decide how to get the man to follow my instructions. Sometimes we have to raise our

continues...

voices to command authority. When I knew that the baby could possibly be born in the vehicle and slide down her pant leg and suffocate or the driver get distracted and cause a wreck, I had to be a little more forceful. If we yell at you, know that it's only to get your attention and help you. Especially those of us who have done the job for awhile, we know how to be stubborn when we are right!

CHICKEN AND RICE CASSEROLE

by Missy

My family loves this recipe. If everything doesn't fit into 1 large casserole dish, put the overage into a small one for leftovers!

Prep Time: **20 min.** | Cook Time: **45 min @ 350° F**

INGREDIENTS

- 1 (10¾ oz.) can Cream of Celery Soup
- 1 (10¾ oz.) can Cream of Chicken Soup
- 1 small bag Frozen Chopped Carrots
- 1 small bag Frozen Peas
- 6 c. Cooked Diced Chicken
- 1 small jar Mayonnaise
- 4 (8.5 oz.) Bags Ben's Original Long Grain Wild Rice
- 2 (8 oz.) bags Shredded Sharp Cheddar Cheese
- 2 small jars Pimento
- ½ c. Dried Onion Flakes
- Pam Spray

INSTRUCTIONS:

1. Preheat oven to 350 degrees
2. Boil Chicken and dice it into bite size pieces
3. Microwave the 4 bags of Ben's Original rice individually according to the directions on the bag
4. Microwave the peas and carrots
5. Transfer everything into a large casserole dish and bake at 350° F for about 45 minutes or until bubbly.

Once everything is cooked add everything to a large mixing bowl and mix thoroughly then transfer to large casserole dish.

DOMESTIC ABUSE

by Missy

There is a rumor circulating around that if you call 911 and order pizza, they will send help. That is not true in all cases. People mistakenly call 911 all the time. A child playing on a phone, a misdial, etc. Every time we get an incomplete 911 call we have to call it back--at least our agency does. All you have to do is stay on the line and answer a few questions. No big deal. If we have to call you back, it's just more steps for an overworked dispatcher to do.

But back to that pizza call. A woman called 911 and I, of course, answered the call. She said, "Hello, I'd like to place an order for..." and then proceeded to give me her address. I thought this was strange so I typed in her address and discovered an advisory for domestic abuse at that location. We call them 10-16s in police speak.

I asked her if she knew she had dialed 911, and she answered that she did. I could also hear a man in the background yelling at her to "just order the damn pizza already!" I then verified her address and phone number and told her to say what she would normally say when ordering a pizza and that I was going to ask her yes or no questions. I assured her that the police had been dispatched already.

The types of questions we ask are difficult to put into a "yes" or "no" format. For instance, if we ask: "Does anyone have a weapon?" and they say yes, then I would want to know what kind in order to warn my officers. In this particular instance I did receive an unfortunate "yes."

"Is it a knife?"

"No."

"A gun?"

"Yes."

Perfect. Now I had to find out what kind of gun. A pistol shoots short range, but if he had a rifle, he could fire at my officers from further away. It ended up being a pistol. Did he have it on him? Or was it somewhere in the house easily accessible? Was anyone else in the house with her? (Of course, there had to be children, and children are my weakness. I cannot take it when they are in harm's way.)

By this time the man had become suspicious of why she was on the phone so long. I told her to pretend to hang up but to lay the phone down close so I could hear what was going on. I heard him slap her and say that she better never betray him and call the police. I relayed this information to the responding units, but he didn't yet suspect that she had actually called 911.

Minutes later I heard the doorbell ring and his voice telling her to answer the door. When she opened the door the officers immediately pulled her outside and went in with guns drawn. Fortunately, he was arrested without incident thanks to the desperation and bravery of my pizza-order caller. Too many times women will not press charges against their abuser because they need their partner's money to feed their children. But some women aren't as lucky as this one. She survived. She was smart. I hope she never took him back, but I will never know.

911 Emergency Dispatchers, Public Safety Responders

INCREDIBLE DENIAL

by Missy

It was another late shift evening in the dispatch center. We received a call of a bad accident. All the proper apparatus and police units were dispatched. When they arrived, the driver of the vehicle was in a fetal position with blood coming from his ears. This is known as "posturing," and indicates a traumatic head injury most of the time. A Lifeline helicopter was called. When this happens, dispatch usually provides another operations channel so the landing zone and the helicopter pilot can communicate. The firefighters in charge of helping to land the helicopter at night use ground lighting such as flares or LED lights. When the helicopter is in range, they talk to the landing zone personnel and land safely. By then the patient has usually been extricated and is put in the chopper immediately. If the patient is still not extricated, the helicopter idles until they receive the patient and fly to an appropriate hospital for that particular injury.

Typically an officer will go to the residence registered on the license plate of the vehicle involved in the crash to make a notification of death or injury. On this night, there wasn't enough time. The lead officer asked to find a phone number to the address listed on the license plate of the car. This occurred back when everyone had a landline telephone, which made this process much easier. We had a large book called a Criss Cross. We could look up addresses to find a phone number, which is how I found the phone number in this case.

I called, and a female answered the phone. I asked her if her husband's name was _____ (name reserved for privacy), and she said yes. I asked if he drove the color, make, and model of the car in the accident, and she said yes. I then told her that police officers would like to meet her at Methodist Hospital regarding her husband who was in an accident.

"My husband is in bed, and his car is in the driveway," she replied.

I again repeated what I had said to make sure I had the right person: address, name of the victim, and the color, make, and model of the car. She confirmed but insisted that his car, the same car I described, was in her driveway. I asked her to look again.

"No," she said, "I know it's there."

"Well would you please wake up your husband then?" I asked.

"No," she responded again.

I then looked to my supervisor for what to do next. She told me that I had to tell the woman what happened. Usually we try not to break bad news on the phone. I just wanted her to either call the lead officer or go meet him at Methodist.

So I gently said, "Ma'am, your husband was in a terrible accident involving the car I described to you. His ID has his name listed at the address you just confirmed. The license plate on the car also came back to his name and your address. You need to get to Methodist Hospital if you want to see him. He may not make it."

I felt awful, even sick to my stomach, to have to give her bad news like that. But to my surprise, she called me a liar and hung up on me. I relayed all of this information to the lead officer, and he decided to call himself after he got to the hospital. The male was later pronounced deceased.

I never knew what happened to the wife. Were they fighting, and she thought I was playing a joke? Was she in denial? This is where this job takes its toll. It's like reading a suspenseful book with the last chapter torn out. I was heartbroken for her because after she found out the real truth, she had to feel very sad. I wish I could have comforted her somehow. But I know that I did all I could do at that time.

WARM AND FUZZY

by Missy

It was early in my career when I took a memorable 911 call during second shift (14:00-22:00). A very calm man told me his son was choking. Being fairly new, I was scared for this poor child! So I started a call for help and indicated "choking person" as the call type. Then I proceeded to ask questions and give instructions to the man to help his son.

I asked how old the child was. He didn't know.

I asked if it was an infant, a boy, or a teen. He said he didn't know!

By then, I was telling medics and police to step it up because I knew something wasn't right. I used every technique I was taught to try and get information from this man and tell him how to help his choking son, but he just kept rambling about himself. I finally had to verbally slap him - a technique we use where we raise our voice to get someone's attention.

"Sir! You are going to listen to me to help your son! Where is he?"

He answered, "I don't have a son!"

While I was feeling utterly bewildered and trying to get my bearings, the caller told me that I made him feel "warm and fuzzy," and then he giggled.

It was no surprise, then, when the police finally arrived and advised medics to stand down because the man in question was "10-56" - which means, of course, "intoxicated." A search of the entire house revealed that he was there alone. No son in sight, choking or otherwise.

I felt so relieved to hear those deputies tell me that no one was choking. And I also could never hear the phrase "warm and fuzzy" again without feeling uneasy!

MEATBALL AND SAUSAGE NIBBLERS

by Missy

INGREDIENTS

2 bags Lil Smokies Sausages

2 lbs. Hamburger

1 Egg

½ or a 15 oz. can of Bread Crumbs

1/2 c. diced onions

1 (18 oz.) jars Peach or Apricot Preserves

1 (20 oz.) cans Canned Chunk Pineapple

2 (18 oz.) bottles BBQ Sauce

INSTRUCTIONS:

1. Mix Hamburger, egg, bread crumbs, dried onions. Roll into balls and cook in a frying pan until done.
2. Add everything to the crockpot and cook on high for 2 hours
3. then put on low.

 Serve when ready

*You can substitute frozen meatballs or use the recipe to make your own.

MONKEY

by Missy

One summer day in the dispatch center, my co-worker and I each took simultaneous 911 calls. Her call was from a person inside a house; mine was from a person outside a house. We soon discovered that it was the same house. We were seated side by side, so we could hear each other trying to calm the callers and find out what was going on. My co-worker was talking to a boy inside the house whose friend had been injured by their pet monkey, named Eujo. I was taking a call from the mother of the household, who had managed to get outside. Apparently the monkey had escaped through a faulty cage door and was loose in their house. Their children had overnight guests, and Eujo  had scratched a 15-year-old male on the head and also bit the ear of the family dog. The kids had managed to lock themselves in a room to get away from Eujo. The 15-year-old male was bleeding and needed medical attention. We start the appropriate responses: Fire (they respond on medical calls also), Police, Paramedics, and EMS. My co-worker was giving instructions to the kids on how to control the bleeding, and I was reassuring the mother that her children were receiving help and were safely locked in another room. Her husband was also outside, and I could hear him in the background pounding on windows and rattling the outside part of Eujo's cage, screaming for him to get back inside his enclosure.

The deputies responding to the call had asked me to discover, if possible, what type of monkey and then look it up on the internet to tell them how big it was and how fast it could run. The caller informed me that it was a Patas Monkey, about 40 pounds. According to the internet, they could run up to 34 miles per hour. The deputies were talking on car-to-car and trying to form a plan of action. One of them used to be a dispatcher who I had helped train when he was just starting out, before he became a deputy. His plan was just to try and run faster than one other deputy. I had to work hard not to giggle over the phone about that as I turned my attention back to the caller.

The Medics, EMS, and Fire had arrived, but they have to "stage" away from the house, meaning they cannot approach the scene until the police secure the scene and advise it is safe. My caller wanted me to ask the ambulance if they had any lollipops. I thought maybe the shock was getting to her, so I asked her to explain. She said Eujo liked lollipops and maybe they could lure him with one.

So I keyed up on the radio for medics and EMS personnel: "Does anyone have a lollipop?"

"Control, is there a diabetic patient?" they replied.

"Negative," I advised, and had to explain the situation. But no one had any lollipops.

The police had arrived by that time, and the caller's husband had managed to coax Eujo to his outdoor enclosure. It was attached to the house so he could go inside and outside. The medics attended to the injured 15-year-old, and the strange situation ended well.

It wasn't until hanging up the call that I recalled what the woman kept saying to me on the phone: "Eujo is just like a child to me, like one of my own kids, like I gave birth to him. I can't believe he is acting like this!" Everything was a bit chaotic from talking on the radio and giving the police and medics information about the monkey, so I didn't process those words while on the phone with her. It is probably good that I didn't have to respond to them during a live call! The experience was certainly the kind of call that a dispatcher never forgets.

HOT GERMAN POTATO SALAD

by Missy

You can also double this and put in a crockpot to keep warm if you want to make it ahead.

Prep Time: 30 min

INGREDIENTS

- 6 lg. Potatoes
- 1 pkg. Thick Bacon
- 1 lg. Onion (chopped)
- ½ c. Red Wine Vinegar
- ½ c. Water
- ½ c. Sugar

INSTRUCTIONS:

1. Leaving the skins on the potatos, cut them in cubes and boil with skins on until tender
2. Fry Bacon to a crispy brown and when cooled, break into pieces
3. Saute chopped onion in the bacon grease until translucent
4. Put these ingredients in a serving bowl and pour the rest of the ingredients over the potato, onions and bacon.

Mix the vinegar, sugar and water for the dressing for the salad.

CHICKEN VELVET SOUP

by Missy

If you want a bit of a hot kick, add cayenne pepper or some hot sauce. Can be added to the whole pot or just let each person determine their level of heat. Another add on is Cheese!

Prep Time: **30 min.** | *Cook Time:* **40 min.**

INGREDIENTS

- 6 Tbsp. Butter
- ⅓ cup Flour
- ½ cup Cream
- ½ cup Milk
- 3 cups Chicken Broth
- 1 ½ cups Chicken, Cooked and Diced

INSTRUCTIONS:

1. Melt butter
2. Blend in Flour
3. Add milk, cream and broth
4. Cook to a boil
5. Reduce heat
6. Add Chicken
7. Heat to a boil again
8. Salt and Pepper to taste

911 Emergency Dispatchers, Public Safety Responders

TRANSLATOR

by Missy

Occasionally police officers or firefighters or medics would take a part-time job in Dispatch on their days off. Ideally, like all full-time and part-time dispatchers, they were supposed to know how to work every console. But firefighters would often pout if they didn't get the fire console. Nowadays the dispatch center likes to split into call takers, police dispatchers, and fire/EMS dispatchers. I was lucky because when I started as a dispatcher I got to work all the consoles.

On one particular occasion I was training a firefighter who had taken a part-time position as a dispatcher. He had advanced to a point that he could sit at a console without me, but I was available for any questions. He took a call from a non-English speaking man whom he could not understand. The trainee put the man on hold and asked me what to do. I told him about the Language Line resource where they provide a translator in any language to assist our callers. Sometimes it takes a few minutes to find a translator, but it is a very valuable tool to have.

When I asked my trainee which language the caller spoke, he said, "Spanish." I started explaining the process of getting a translator, but he said that he had a better idea:

"There's a guy on duty at my fire station right now who speaks Spanish. I will get him on the line and save the county some money on the translator!"

So he went through the process of getting a three-way line going to his fire station and asked for his Spanish-speaking friend, who said he would be happy to help. The friend started talking to the caller in Spanish, but after listening to the caller for a minute he said, "Dude, this guy is Russian! I can't help him!"

I had picked up the line, too, to listen in, but I had to hang up because I was laughing so hard! How could this trainee mistake Russian for Spanish?

We finally got the caller to the Language Line, found him a translator, and dispatched an officer to unlock his car, which turned out to be the simple reason for his call. Thank goodness it wasn't anything serious! My trainee was, of course, extremely embarrassed. Especially when his battalion chief called dispatch laughing because the Spanish-speaking friend told everyone at the fire department about his faux pas.

Even now, whenever I hear someone speaking Russian, I wonder if that was our caller. And I wonder what he thought of his experience with a highly trained firefighter who had a very bad ear for languages.

I may have upset an officer for not pulling over for him because I knew I wasn't speeding. I had told him his hair was receding and as I went to get food, he tried to pull me over. I just drove back to our parking lot. He fake yelled at me and this is what I came out to after my shift. My car is the silver Ford Escape. Missy Birnell Haston.

HORSE

by Missy

It was a hot and humid July 4th, on a Friday that year, when I took a call from an earnest woman whose horse had died. The caller informed me that the renderer, who picks up large deceased animals, could not come and get the horse since it was a holiday weekend. I was curious why this person had called emergency dispatch for their dilemma. Well, the caller wanted to know if burning the horse was allowed since the body was too big to bury and Monday was too far away to wait for pick-up.

I was caught off guard, not surprisingly. One does not expect to get a call in the dispatch center for permission to set a beloved large deceased ("10-0" in police jargon) pet on fire. Nor is that in any training scenario. So I told the caller I would get in touch with the fire battalion chief for her area and get back with her. Then I called the battalion chief and explained the unusual inquiry. After a few laughs and groans, we discovered that the caller's address was actually a county address, so the burn ordinance technically did not apply to them.

"Put me through to the caller," he said.

I, of course, stayed on the line to eavesdrop - a privilege that I felt I had earned by patching him through to the caller instead of making him write the number down and call on his own.

The battalion chief and caller exchanged pleasantries, and then the chief began explaining that although legally they could burn the body, they lived across the street from a subdivision that did have a burn ordinance. So if anyone complained of the smoke or the smell, the fire department would have to respond and extinguish the fire.

"Well, where would that leave me then?" the woman asked.

Without missing a beat the battalion chief responded: "With a half burned horse."

It took all my willpower to keep from laughing out loud, and even still the chief could tell over the line that I was barely holding it in. The laugh we shared afterwards was almost as good as the ones I had to stifle.

HOMEMADE GUACAMOLE

by Missy

Prep Time: **20 min**.

INGREDIENTS

4 Ripe Avocados

1 Red Onion, minced

1 Bunch Fresh Cilantro Leaves (Chopped)

2 Tbsp. Lime Juice

Black Pepper, to taste

Sea Salt, to taste

1 sm. Container Grape Tomatoes, halved

1 or 2 Serrano Pepper, Chopped (optional)

INSTRUCTIONS:

1. Mash avocados with a potato masher. Mix in the rest of the ingredients.
2. Serve with Tortilla chips

NOTES:

Serrano peppers are hot. Only chop with a knife and wash hands after chopping. Remember, these are optional only if you want it spicy.

QUICKSAND

by Missy

One typical afternoon in the dispatch center began as any normal day with usual calls - such as: "Why is there not an officer directing traffic at my child's school?" and "I am not from around here; can you tell me how to get to Walmart?"

I sat at my console, expecting the same types of calls to continue but always ready for a true emergency as we dispatchers must be. Then a 911 call came through my line.

"911, what's the address of your emergency?" I said, as I pulled up the call.

On the other end of the line I heard a tiny voice. The child sounded about four or five years old. Typically 911 calls from a child this age are for one of two reasons: a complete false alarm or a severe emergency. We always assume first that it is a true emergency.*

This child was audibly in some distress as he stated, "My mommy is sinking."

My mind immediately went to drowning, so while fearing it was quite serious but talking reassuringly to the child, I also started medics, police, and firefighters to the location.

The child was not crying or otherwise acting as if he was in great fear, but he was absolutely adamant that his mother was sinking. I asked him if she was inside or outside, and he said, "Outside." This turned my thoughts toward a swimming pool.

"What is your mommy sinking in?" I asked.

"Quicksand," the little voice replied.

That definitely caught me off guard! But I could now hear a female in the background, and she did sound like she needed help. She was not screaming or hysterical, but her voice was high-pitched, unrestrained, guttural. Hearing her voice reassured me, though, that this probably was not a swimming pool or drowning situation. That was a relief! I continued relaying new information to the responders en route.

Even though the 911 CAD call had shown a location and address, we always try to verify the information with the caller. I asked the child if he lived in a neighborhood with houses around him, and he said yes. So that ruled out my grain silo sinking theory.

"Do you have a sand pile or some mulch that maybe your mommy climbed up and is sinking in?" I asked him.

"No," he said. He kept insisting it was quicksand.

At this point the voice in the background grew more distinct, sounding like maybe the child was moving closer to his mom. I heard the mother now saying to the child, "Toss me the phone but don't come any closer."

The child obeyed his mother, and I was finally on the line with the person in distress. I could barely understand her. She seemed hysterical.

"Ma'am, ma'am, this is 911 dispatch. Help is on the way. Please calm down and tell me what is going on," I told her.

She took a moment to catch her breath and then said, "I am not in danger. But I am stuck and sinking…..in mud."

Her hysterics that I had heard were from laughing at her poor child who was so worried about her. Their house was a new one, with no grass, and rain had created a pool of mud in her backyard. She had mud up over her knees, and the more she tried to get out, the more she sank. So she did need help, but not from sinking in quicksand.

I updated everyone en route, and they all proceeded but now non-signal 10 (without lights and sirens). She told me that she was so embarrassed, but I assured her that we encounter these kinds of situations every day.

"No way," she said.

"Okay, you're right," I told her. "I've never taken a call about quicksand before!"

We both laughed until the help arrived. When they did, it took the firefighters' ropes and ladders plus manpower from the police to pull her out of the mud. She reassured her child that she was fine, and everything turned out great. Except for her boots. Unfortunately they perished in the mud. The crews went back muddy but happy that the situation was not a serious emergency - or real quicksand.

I want to commend any parents who have taught their young children how to call 911. Over the years I have taken many calls from children, one as young as three years old.

SUICIDES

by Missy

I have taken quite a few calls when a person's family member or friend have been found deceased. I can't possibly remember them all, but I do have a few that have stuck with me.

I took a call from a man who stated that two teenage girls who lived next door came to his house because their mother had hung herself. I advised him to leave the girls outside and to go and check if she could be cut down and revived. I started the police and firefighters and emergency medical personnel. The girls were of course hysterical in the background, and I can still hear their cries. My heart ached for them, and I even felt angry at the mother for doing this to her children--but who can really judge what goes on in the mind of another person.

The neighbor went into the house and confirmed that there was a woman hanging from an upstairs bannister. He stated that she was stiff and blue, but he would try to cut her down--as soon as he was able to collect himself. Fortunately, however, an officer arrived just in time and so he was instead able to go and comfort the girls.

The mother was beyond resuscitation. The medics called it on the scene--a paramedic being the only person that is able to pronounce someone deceased. Not an officer, not a regular firefighter, unless it's obvious: decapitation, rigor mortis, decomposition, etc.

The next call like this that I remember was when a worker at an industrial plant found a male coworker of his who had hung himself in a barn. This discovery left him in shock, and I had to verbally slap him (i.e., raise my voice) to get his attention. I felt awful, but I needed to know if we could save him. He said he was in a very tall barn and was on a short rope hanging from the rafters, and that it would take him a while to climb up to the rafters to get up there. He told me the subject was blue, and I advised him not to put himself in danger.

Fire arrived and went to work, but he was already gone. They believed that it occurred the previous night after work.

An overdose is my next memory. It was another mother, but this time the mother didn't want her children to find her. There was a note on the door for the children after school to go to the neighbors house and call the police. She had locked all the doors and windows and had placed foil on her bedroom window, just in case the kids tried to peek in.

As always, everyone that I dispatched arrived and the cause of death was determined as a suicide by overdose. She had waited until her children went to school and then took a large amount of pills. I can't help but wonder how those kids made it through such a tragedy. They weren't teenagers, but they weren't little children either.

These types of calls leave you feeling helpless. All I can do is stay on the line and comfort the callers until help arrives. Of course, after these calls we still have to finish our shift and keep answering the phones or radios. I have to keep my voice calm, compose myself, and answer the next emergency line: "911, what is the exact location of your emergency?"

SALSA MEATLOAF

by Missy

I was bored one day and out of things to cook. I used to hate meatloaf. I looked in my cabinets to see what I could put with hamburger and the idea of putting salsa in it came to me. I also saw a jar of tomato paste and instead of ketchup on top, I tried it. It is now a fancier dish to serve!

Prep Time: **20 min.** | Cook Time: **45 min**

INGREDIENTS

- 2 lbs. Hamburger
- 9 oz. Bread Crumbs
- 1 Egg
- 16 oz. Mild or Hot Salsa
- 1 pkg. Lipton Onion Soup
- 1 (8 oz.) can Tomato Paste

INSTRUCTIONS:

1. Mix hamburger with everything except the tomato paste.
2. Put aluminum foil on a cookie sheet.
3. Put hamburger mixture on the sheet and shape into a loaf.
4. Use the tomato paste on top, like icing a cake. It keeps everything juicy inside.
5. Preheat oven to 375 degrees
6. Cook for about 45 minutes, until a toothpick come out clean
7. If the tomato paste starts to turn dark, and the meat isn't done yet, cover loosely with foil until meat is done.

HAULING ASS

by Missy

I was working a "town" dispatch one morning and saw an animal complaint come across my screen. Then it was changed to a driving complaint - and then back to an animal complaint. I didn't know what to make of it! At this time we were a larger center, usually with 12 dispatchers. There would be one dispatcher managing four police channels, two to three dispatchers dedicated to taking calls, a headquarters dispatcher who verified warrants and answered the phone, a supervisor who also answered the phones, a dedicated fire-only dispatcher, a fire control dispatcher, and two fire back-up dispatchers. I was assigned to taking general calls that day when this strange complaint came through.

The complaint indicated that there was a truck driving on a highway through the town with a donkey tied down in the back. A donkey? I knew this was going to get good.

So, I hit the talk button and said, "Fishers, beat one, copy a driving/animal complaint, southbound 37, passing 146th street. A white Ford 4-door truck with a donkey tied down in the truck bed." One of my favorite officers radioed back: "I am en route to the hauling ass call." I was laughing so hard that I could only manage a mic click to acknowledge him.

Pretty soon I could hear the other officers on their car-to-car radios jumping in with all kinds of other call options:

"Illegal tying down ass."

"Hauling ass over a county line."

"No asses can ride in the back of a truck."

The phrase "hauling ass" took on new meaning for me that day, and it will always be what I think of when I hear those words.

CRUNCHY TUNA CASSEROLE

by Missy

This is my mother Jean Ann Layman Birnell's Recipe. I hated it as a child, but love it now :)

Prep Time: **15 min.** | Cook Time: **30 min** | Oven: **350° f**

INGREDIENTS

- 1 can Cream of Chicken or Mushroom
- ½ can Evaporated Milk
- 1 (5 oz.) Can Tuna
- ¼ c. Onion, chopped
- 1 c. Celery, chopped
- ½ c. Water Chestnuts
- 1 (5 oz.) Can Chow Mein Noodles
- Salt and Pepper to taste

INSTRUCTIONS:

1. Mix soup and milk in a mixing bowl.
2. Add tuna, water chestnuts, celery, and onion.
3. Add ¾ of the can of chow mein noodles.
4. Mix together and cover with the rest of the noodles.
5. Transfere to a casserole dish sprayed with PAM
6. Back at 350 degrees for 25-30 minutes
7. Microwave the 4 bags of Ben's Original rice individually according to the directions on the bag
8. Microwave the peas and carrots
9. Transfer everything into a large casserole dish and bake at 350° F for about 45 minutes or until bubbly.

911 Emergency Dispatchers, Public Safety Responders

DISPATCHER BIO

Cindy DeVaney Robison. I was born in 1969 in Noblesville, Indiana, to Sarah and Silas Devaney. I have a younger brother, Silas III. I grew up in Sheridan, Indiana, which is a small rural community known for their high school football. Go Blackhawks!

In 6th grade, we moved to a house in the country. We had horses, ducks, rabbits, dogs, cats and some goats. My brother and I showed horses locally and in 4-H during our junior high and high school years. I was a 10-year 4-H member and made a lot of friendships and great memories. 4-H taught me many things that are still useful today, and I will always cherish that experience.

After graduation in 1987, I knew college was not for me. I never really liked school and didn't see the need for spending lots of money for something that I didn't like and didn't know what I wanted to study. I worked a couple different jobs, got an apartment with my best friend, and enjoyed the new freedom of adulthood. I also hung out with friends at the Westfield Fire Department. There was only one station at the time because the county hadn't started growing yet. They still had volunteers at the time, so I got to ride along on some calls. That's when I got the bug for public safety.

I became a 911 dispatcher in 1990. It was a small center, and there were 14 dispatchers. It was the most exciting time of my life. We dispatched for the sheriff's department and a few of the small towns and fire departments at that time. It gave me the confidence I didn't have in school. I felt like I was important. I knew all the "stuff" going on in the county. I knew the details of crimes. I knew about robberies, murders, terrible accidents, and big fires. It was fun when friends would ask me if I knew what was going on during a certain night at whatever location, although I could only give vague answers. I worked almost any overtime I could, and when I was not working I would ride along with officers. It was exciting!

I met my husband, Jon, at work, and we were married in 1994. He is the great love of my life. He had two children, Ben and Emily. Eventually we ended up working the same shift for over 20 years. Unless there was a huge event or a funny event, we never really talked about work at home, but we understood each other's jobs. We were a team. He retired in 2021 with 31 years on the road. Congratulations, Jon!

My retirement is around the corner, too. In my career as a dispatcher, I have made lifelong friends, watched their kids grow up, and been to weddings and funerals. And I wouldn't change a thing.

Cindy in the old dispatch center in the early 90's.

BANANA BREAD

by Cindy

Prep Time: **15 min.** | Cook Time: **60 min.** | Oven Temp: **350°F**

INGREDIENTS

- 1 ½ c. Ripe Bananas
- 2 lg. Eggs
- ½ c. Applesauce, unsweetened
- ⅓ c. Honey or Maple Syrup
- 3 Tbsp. Coconut or Avocado Oil
- 1 tsp. each Vanilla extract and or Almond Extract
- 2 tsp. Baking Powered
- 1 tsp. Baking Soda
- ¼ tsp. Salt, less is fine
- 2 ¼ c. Flour, Whole Wheat or your choice
- ¼ tsp. Cinnamon, optional

INSTRUCTIONS:

1. In a large bowl, mash the bananas. eggs, applesauce, honey or maple syrup, oil, vanilla or almond extract, baking powder, baking soda and salt;
2. Whisk to combine (a masher works well).
3. Add flour and stir gently to mix. (add cinnamon if desired)
4. Preheat oven to 350°F. Use a 9 x 5" loaf pan. You can either oil the surface of the pan or use parchment paper as a lining.
5. Pour the mixed batter in the loaf pan and bake for 45 to 60 minutes.
6. Check with fork or toothpick, when it comes out clean, you're ready to eat.
7. Remove from the oven and let cool for a few minutes, remove from the pan.
8. Cut into slices and serve.

Lisa and Cindy posing with Officer Carey's statue. He is the only police officer in Carmel killed in the line of duty. It happened in 1900.

PAT DOWN

by Cindy

In the early days of my career in dispatch, we were connected to the jail, with a very large window in between. There were only two female correction officers at the time. One worked first shift (6 a.m. - 2 p.m.), and the other worked second shift (2 p.m. - 10 p.m.).

If a female was being brought to the jail during third shift, or if the officers had a day off or a vacation, then a female dispatcher would need to pat down any female prisoners before they entered. One night I was tasked with patting down a drunk female. The sally port was basically a four-car garage with overhead doors on either side - and not particularly bright lighting either.

For the pat down, I went into the sally port where the woman was and started at the top with her collar, then continued to move down. I reached the pockets on her pants and then had to check her legs, including her inseam. I was in for a surprise! When my hands felt wet material, I realized that she had wet her pants. No one had told me in advance. I never performed a pat down again without gloves on!

CARDBOARD CUTOUT

by Cindy

At the dispatch center, the strangest calls inevitably come at the busiest times. That was certainly the case for one particular 911 call that I took from an alarmed woman. She had called to say that she was house sitting for a friend who was on vacation and when she went upstairs to retrieve some towels, she saw a man standing in the hallway. He was wearing a suit and staring at her! She was quite disturbed, being alone at a strange house.

County deputies came to the rescue and checked the house, beginning upstairs. They did, in fact, find a man in a suit standing in the hallway.

That is, if you can call a life-size cardboard cutout a "man."

SPARING DUMMY

by Cindy

The things that help us keep a sense of humor as dispatchers may not be average office humor. But in an environment that can be very stressful and sad at times, we take laughter wherever we can find it. One particular call gave us a good laugh and some much needed stress relief.

The call came in while we were really busy. A woman called to say that a man was standing in their barn. She immediately ran back to the house to call 911. We dispatched two county deputies. They checked the perimeter of the barn, and everything seemed okay. They went inside to check and found
a man standing in the barn, just like the caller said! They gave verbal commands, but there was no response from him. They moved closer and closer to the subject, until they were close enough to realize that their subject was really just a sparing dummy. The woman's husband had put it in the barn but didn't tell his wife.

One of the deputies texted me a picture of the "man" in the barn, and we all enjoyed a laugh.

CAMPING PUMPKIN PIE

by Cindy

This trail-ready version is good as the real thing, and very portable for hikers and campers. Enjoy !!!

Prep Time: **20 min.** | Cook Time: **20 min.** | Oven Temp: **350°F**

INGREDIENTS

2 tsp. Pumpkin Pie Spice
2 tsp. Sugar
4 Tbsp. Butter, Melted
1 c. Graham Crackers, crushed
Marshmallows, to your taste.

INSTRUCTIONS:

CRUST To make your crust.

1. Combine your crushed graham crackers and melted butter, mix till everything is moistened.
2. Press down in a skillet or pie pan.

FILLING To make your filling.

1. Combine your pumpkin pie spice and your sugar, with your canned pumpkin in a sauce pan, just heat till warm.
2. Pour your pumpkin filling into the crust. Top with toasted marshmallows.
3. If you are at home: take your marshmallow topped pie and put in the oven to toast your marshmallows. About 10 minutes, keep an eye out, they will burn quickly. If you are camping; After you have your filling poured in your pie crust, toast some marshmallows over the campfire, and spread on the pie.

MISCARRIAGE

by Cindy

During one dispatch shift, I received a 911 call from an elderly woman who was rather panicked. She told me that she was hemorrhaging. I started asking the normal questions for hemorrhage when she told me that she was having a miscarriage. For a moment I was confused, because of her age. She was so convincing. She wanted me to call her husband to come home. He was working across the street in his office, in a big office building, she said "The address that came up for the caller was a nursing home, and looking on the map I could tell that there was not a big office building across the street.

So, I realized that she was remembering her miscarriage from many years ago. I'm not sure if she had dementia or Alzheimer's, but it broke my heart for her. She was crying and asking for her husband, probably like she did when it really happened. My partner called the nursing home to send someone down to her room while I continued to talk with her. She was remembering her time in Chicago. Her husband worked in a big office building, and she just wanted him with her. Her emotions were real, and I felt so sorry for her because she was reliving probably one of the worst days of her life. She was very sweet, and I just went with her story and treated it like she was having a miscarriage. I think about her often, and I hope she is at peace.

SOMEONE STOLE MY SPICE

by Cindy

It was a pretty slow day in dispatch when I took a 911 call from a younger male who was very upset. I assumed it was going to be a car crash or someone gravely ill, judging by his tone.

"Someone stole my spice!" he said, to my surprise.

I was confused. So I asked him, "What kind of spice?"

"You know, SPICE!" he replied.

"Do you mean like salt and pepper?" I said.

"No, no, no," he answered, and then tried to explain to me that it was a drug similar to marijuana.

This was the first we had heard of spice, when it was first being sold at gas stations and before it became illegal. I'm not even sure if the guys on the road were aware of it yet. We all got a good laugh about how this man was so upset because someone stole his "spice" - and how I was so confused!

HEALTHY ZUCCHINI BREAD

by Cindy

Prep Time: **10 min.** | Cook Time: **60 min.** | Oven Temp: **350°F**

INGREDIENTS

2 c. Zucchini, grated, packed and not squeezed

1 lg. Egg

½ c. Unsweetened Apple Sauce

¾ c. Raw Honey or Maple Syrup

2 tsp. Cinnamon

1 tsp. Vanilla Extract

2 c. Flour, Whole Wheat or Spelt

1 tsp. Baking Soda

2 tsp. Baking Powder

½ tsp. Salt

Cooking Spray to taste

INSTRUCTIONS:

1. In a large mixing bowl, add egg, applesauce, honey, vanilla, cinnamon, baking soda, baking powder and salt; whisk until combined.
2. Add zucchini and stir
3. Add flour and mix gently with a spatula, just enough to combine.
4. Pour batter in your prepared baking pan.
5. Preheat oven to 350 degrees, line a 9 x 5 load pan with parchment paper and spray with cooking spray and set aside.
6. Pour batter in your loaf pan and bake approximately 1 hour. Insert a toothpick in the center of loaf, loaf is done when it comes out clean.
7. Remove from oven and cool about 10 minutes, Holding the parchment paper flaps, remove the zucchini bread from your pan. Let cool completely before serving.

DISPATCHER BIO

Becky Feltz. Becky has worked in public safety for 22 years: 18 years as a 911 dispatcher and currently as the accounts payable/payroll administrator with a local police department. She is responsible for paying all the department bills and managing their multi-million dollar budget. On occasion, as needed, she also serves as the backup payroll administrator to make sure everyone receives a paycheck. She admits that it can be challenging at times, but enjoys her job.

Early in Becky's career she worked for USA Group. She really didn't like that job or find it fulfilling enough to keep her satisfied, so in 1996 she and her husband took a risk and established their own business - Feltz Masonry, Inc. Becky managed the administrative duties of the business, while her husband was the face of the business. Together they worked as a team and built a successful business from the ground up, until the market crashed in 2007 and they were forced to dissolve it. Being self-employed was enjoyable, but Becky wanted to seek part-time employment outside the home to help pay the bills and get out of the house.

In 1999, she accepted a position as a 911 dispatcher that she thought would be just temporary. She continued to work part time for five years and then became full-time in 2004. During her career as a dispatcher, she received two awards: Riverview Dispatcher of the Year (2005) and the Lifesaver Award (2010). Becky also received several certifications: CPR, IDACS/NCIC, EMD, EFD, and EPD. She became a mobile data dispatch trainer and certified communications training officer. She also received additional training in active shooter and crisis intervention to aid in her abilities to help those in need over the phone. Attending a few public safety conferences helped Becky to refresh, restart, and build on her career within the public safety field. She assisted, alongside others, rewriting and developing the training program established in dispatch that is still used today. Training new dispatchers and giving them the tools and backbone they needed to succeed were some of Becky's favorite aspects of her role. In 2015, she coordinated an appreciation event during National Telecommunications Week for all of her co-workers, she took pride in planning it and making others happy. Later in her career, Becky became a supervisor in dispatch. She was responsible for payroll, monitoring the overtime budget, and tracking employee benefit time. She generated the work schedule for her shift to maintain appropriate coverage needed for the center and organized the mandatory overtime schedule when necessary. Becky assisted in processing tape requests for officers, management, and prosecutors (everything in dispatch is recorded and can be used for training and court if needed). At times she would document both good and bad events in guardian tracking for her subordinates and also implemented a performance improvement plan for those in need. Becky was considered a great asset to dispatch and her team. In 2016, Becky decided to leave her 911 job and further her career within public safety. She accepted a job with a local police department, where she remains today. She loves her job and attributes her success to everything she learned as a 911 dispatcher.

Becky graduated high school from Hamilton Heights in the small town of Arcadia, Indiana. After high school, she attended Ball State University for accounting. She only attended college for two and a half years before she met the love of her life, and they decided to start a family together. Choosing to concentrate on her new baby boy, she did not return to college to finish her degree at that time. Becky started taking classes again in 2014 to slowly earn her bachelor's degree in Business Administration with a concentration in Accounting. While working full-time she admits this is not an easy task, but she only has a few more classes and hopes to be finished by the end of 2023.

Becky has been married for 27 years to a wonderful husband who still shows his love for her every day. They have three amazing boys together who are all grown and married with their own families. She has gained three beautiful daughter-in-laws and four adorable grandchildren. She and her husband have dedicated their lives to their family and love them all dearly.

CAKE BALLS

by Becky

You can also do these on lollipop sticks to make cake pops. These were very popular with everyone in dispatch. I made them several times and became very good at it. I eventually started a side business making them for all kinds of people.

Prep Time: **2-3 hours.** | Cook Time: **15-18 min @ 350° F**

INGREDIENTS

- 1 box Cake Mix, any flavor (18.25 oz size)
- Eggs - per box instruction
- Oil - per box instruction
- Water - per box instruction
- 16 oz. Ready made Frosting, any flavor
- ½ c. Sprinkles (optional)
- 1 pkg. Almond Bark

INSTRUCTIONS:

1. Prepare cake mix as directed on box. Prepare a 9 x 13" pan - spray with cooking spray.
2. Bake cake for 15-18 minutes or until golden. (insert toothpick, should come out dry)
3. Let cake cool completely- then crumble in a large bowl.
4. Stir in ¼ c. frosting mixing with your hands to form a dough mixture. (use more or less frosting as needed, but don't make it to sticky)
5. Roll 1 ½ inch balls and place on cookie sheet with parchment paper.
6. Chill in refrigerator for 1 hour.
7. While balls are chilling, melt almond bark in microwave in 30 second increments, stirring in between, until chocolate is smooth.
8. Place one ball on a fork and dip down in chocolate until coated. shake off any excess chocolate and place ball back on parchment paper on cookie sheet.
9. Top with sprinkles while chocolate is still wet- let them dry completely and serve.

SHOTS FIRED

by Becky

Working as a 911 dispatcher is not like any regular 8 a.m.- 5 p.m. job. One of the main reasons is that you never know what's going to happen during your shift. We are all trained for many different situations and scenarios, but until they actually happen to you, you never know how you're going to react or handle them. One that I will never forget is the day I heard the words "Shots fired; dispatch shots fired!"

I don't remember what day of the week it was, but when I walked into work, I knew I was on dispatch 1 - a radio channel that is responsible for telling officers where to respond to and helps the dispatchers keep all the officers on that channel safe throughout a shift. The dispatch 1 channel would have approximately 15-18 officers to keep track of, and they would consist of officers from five municipalities, hospital security, and courthouse security. I remember going through our shift change talks: what's going on, who is on what call, and what's pending, if anything. I remember logging into the CAD (computer aided dispatch) and checking to make sure my CAD information matched what I was told from the previous person. I would double and triple check everything and everyone. Mistakes were just not an option with this job.

The morning was just getting started when the startled voice screamed out over the radio, "Shots fired; dispatch, shots fired!" My body tensed up, and I started to sweat a little (I do that when I get nervous). I knew at that moment that I had to rely on my training and react quickly to get as much information as I could and get help to him FAST because every second counts. They didn't give me a unit number, but each radio is pre-programmed to who it belongs to in case of emergencies, like this one. I immediately noticed it was from courthouse security, so I keyed up my radio:

"Attention all units, shots fired at the courthouse, shots fired at the courthouse. Any unit to start that way for assistance" (you always repeat yourself in case they missed any of it the first time, it's part of our training).

I had several units mark 10-76 "en route." By "several" I mean everyone on duty and then some! Now that I had units started that way, I wanted to get more information to help them know how and exactly where to respond when they got there.

I keyed back up on my radio and said, "Is there any unit at the courthouse that can provide a location and status?"

A different security officer gave a location where he presumed it happened and who he believed was involved. I called a "signal 100" on my dispatch channel, which means the only radio traffic allowed was anything involving that particular event, and I continued to mark units on scene with their exact locations given. I remember it took a while to get everyone on the call and the CAD updated, but my teammates were there to help. Help arrived quickly, and they soon marked "one in custody" and "scene secure." I released the signal 100 and just like that for me, it was over!

I continued to dispatch other calls and take traffic stops, like any other routine day. We don't always get to stop and take a moment to reflect on things that happen. We have to continue on with call after call because that's our job. It was finally time to go home, so at shift change I passed along all the events from my day, what was currently going on, who was where, and what was pending, and finally walked away. At that moment I had to know if that officer was ok. I was able to ask a couple of officers as I was leaving if everyone was alright from the courthouse incident. I learned that there was one officer injured, but he would be ok. At home that evening I remember going through the events in my head and wondering what I could have done differently or should have done differently. Then I remembered: HE WAS GOING TO BE OK! My shift was a success. I knew I had to work the next day, and immediately started to wonder what tomorrow would bring.

911 Emergency Dispatchers, Public Safety Responders

DISPATCHER OF THE YEAR AWARD

by Becky

I can vividly recall events from a 911 call I took back in 2005. I know most people can't remember what they did a year or even a month ago, remember what they had for dinner a week ago, or remember details from a phone call they had a few nights ago, but most people doesn't have to endure phone call after phone call of tragic events that will forever haunt them. When I signed up as a 911 dispatcher, I had no idea the things I would later hear and never be able to forget, or the feelings I would have for those who were involved in tragic accidents. The memories of good and bad that will be forever stuck in my head - But I loved my job and wouldn't change that part of my life for anything.

In 2005, I answered a 911 call for help from someone who found a canoe that had capsized in the White River. He didn't see anyone around at first but then quickly saw a young lifeless child in the water. He rapidly pulled the child inside his boat and was frantically waiting for any directions from me. I was only on the call a few seconds before I asked if he could listen for any air movement or see the chest rise up and down. I needed to know if the child was breathing.

"No, he's not breathing," the caller said.

"Then we are going to start CPR," I directed. "I will walk you through it."

"I don't think that will help," he replied. "I think he's already gone."

I repeated the directive to start CPR, knowing that we needed to give this child a chance, but the caller continued to refuse because of the lifeless body already lying there. I wanted to yell and scream at him because I couldn't imagine anyone not wanting to try and save a life - a child's life! I quickly became frustrated but knew I couldn't give up. I knew I had to come up with something else fast.

"Did you see the canoe capsize?" I asked him, trying a new angle.

"No, I did not," he replied.

"Do you have any children, sir?" I inquired.

"Yes", he replied.

"Wouldn't you want someone to do the same thing for your children if they were ever in this situation?" I said. "Since you didn't see the canoe capsize, we have no idea how long this child has been in the water, so every minute is critical. We HAVE to start CPR right away to give him a fighting chance."

I was relieved to hear him finally say, "Ok, what do I do first?"

Everyone has a specific responsibility in the dispatch center. There is someone assigned to take calls, someone to dispatch police calls to the officers, and then someone else assigned to dispatch fire & EMS calls to the appropriate apparatus. My partners had already started police and EMS to the scene, so I assured the caller there was help already on the way (you might wonder why the police were started since there was no criminal activity, but the police can usually get there much faster than a medic can, and they carry AED's - automated external defibrillator), and they are trained professionals.

I started to give him step-by-step instructions to perform CPR. He was doing everything I asked him to do and continued the 15 compressions to 2 breaths over and over and over and over for about 5 -7 minutes. Help soon arrived, and they were able to take over and treat the child the best they could.

Unfortunately, I found out the next day that they were not able to save the child. I was emotional and sad to know I lost a child. He wasn't my child, nor did I even know him, but when I answered the call for help, I became involved in his emergency. The child's dad was also in that canoe and drowned that day too. There was so much tragedy for that family, and I thought about them often for several weeks after that.

I'm not sure how much time had passed after this incident when I received an invitation from Riverview Hospital to attend a banquet. They wanted to give me an award for a 911 call I had taken. They didn't elaborate, so I had no idea what call it could have been; I didn't recall anything special I had done recently or a life I had saved. I went to the banquet and learned it was because of this call. I told them they must have made a mistake because I didn't save anyone. I even reminded them of the horrible outcome. That's when the medical director told me it was because I was persistent, compassionate, and wouldn't take no for an answer until I was able to get the caller to do CPR. I stayed the course, dug deep, and was with the caller every step of the way. I was told it was all of those things that made me stand out. I accepted the Dispatcher of the Year award and said thank you. I still think about that family and all they lost that day. I think about the young boy and what he would have been like today if only he was found sooner. At first I stored the award away in a box so I didn't have to look at it for a long time, but now it sits on my desk at work as a reminder: life is too short!

MY DISPATCH FAMILY

by Becky

When I think of "family" - I think of my grandma, grandpa, mom, dad, sisters, brothers, aunts, uncles, nieces, nephews, and cousins. I think of all these people as part of my immediate family. To me, they are immediate because they are part of my bloodline or lineage (my marriage). My immediate family members are people who I can always count on no matter what. I consider myself one of the lucky ones to have another family, in addition to my immediate family: my Dispatch family. These people are ones who I have worked closely with for many years. We have worked long hours, day after day, and missed out on birthdays and holidays. We've missed our kids playing sports, missed going to cookouts, and even missed out on those relaxing rainy days together. I don't think we all knew what we were signing up for when we applied to be 911 dispatchers, but I can tell you that it has been a ride of a lifetime for most of us.

Inside the dispatch center, it's not always hustle and bustle. There are down times in between the phones ringing and emergencies happening. During those down times, many years ago, we were able to play cards, put puzzles together, or watch movies. It could take us hours or days to get even one of those things done, but we still enjoyed it. I remember working 6 p.m. – 6 a.m., the midnight shift. Once we got through rush hour and dinner hours, things started to slow down, so we all decided to watch a movie. We started thinking about different movies we had access to, and someone would say not any scary movies (that was usually me) or animated movies. It wasn't an easy process, but after talking it out we all finally came to a decision about 2:00 a.m. The movie was getting ready to start when someone said, "Wait a minute! I have to call my husband to see if he's ok with me watching this movie." We all thought she was joking at first, so we started laughing, but then she picked up the phone and started dialing the number. We heard her ask about the movie, tell him what it was about and then hung up the phone. We were all still laughing, but she explained that they watch a lot of movies together so she wanted to make sure he didn't want to see it with her. The same person would also call her husband in the middle of the night to see what he wanted for breakfast, and other random questions any other couple would talk about over dinner. We also played tricks on each other and tried to scare each other.

These were fun days in dispatch.

I remember talking about our kids and things they did growing up - their growing pains, our growing pains. It was nice to have my dispatch family help me through some parenting decisions I had to make. There's no manual on what's right or wrong, so I'm glad they were always there to steer me in the right moral direction. We would also talk about tough times we would have with our significant others. They would share similar things and give great advice. It was just easy with them.

These were good days in dispatch.

We all took our share of emergency calls and dealt with tragic events and deaths. We have heard loud screams and desperate cries on the other end of the phone. We have talked to suicidal people for hours; sometimes we would succeed, and sometimes we wouldn't. We have talked to battered men, women, and children to provide whatever comfort or help we could. We hugged each other and cried together.

These were hard days in dispatch.

No matter what kind of day I had in dispatch, I knew it was going to be ok because I had my dispatch family. Much like my immediate family, I knew they had my back no matter what, and I could count on them for anything. If you are ever lucky enough to be a part of an extended family like I have been, you will understand what I mean. I no longer work in dispatch, but my dispatch family will forever hold a special place in my heart.

MACARONI & CHEESE

by Becky

This is always a favorite for any pitch in. Macaroni and cheese is loved by people of all ages. You can never go wrong when serving this and it's so creamy and cheesy and good.

Prep Time: **20 min.** | *Cook Time:* **1 hr.** | *Oven Temp:* **Crockpot High**

INGREDIENTS

- 1 lb. Elbow macaroni
- 2 c. Milk
- 1 stick Butter
- 8 oz. Sharp Cheddar Cheese, Shredded
- 8 oz. Mild Cheddar Cheese, Shredded
- 1 lb. Velveeta
- 1 can Campbells Cheddar Cheese Soup
- 1 Tbsp. Salt

INSTRUCTIONS:

1. Boil macaroni until almost done. Don't cook to long or it will become mushy.
2. Mix all ingredients together in a crockpot on high until everything is melted - about 30 mins.
3. Add macaroni.
4. Cook in crockpot on medium for about an hour to thicken.
5. Reduce heat to warm - Serve.

CHICKEN FIESTA SOUP

by Becky

I love making this recipe in the fall on a cool day. This was my go to on Halloween because it was easy to throw together.

Prep Time: **30 min.** | *Cook Time:* **3 hrs.** | *Oven Temp:* **Crockpot**

INGREDIENTS

- 4 lg. Boneless Chicken Breast, cooked
- 2 cans Petit Diced Tomatoes w/chilis
- 2 cans Green Beans, Drained
- 1 can Rotell
- 1 can Corn, Drained
- 1 pkg. Brooks Chili Seasoning
- 1 ½ c. Chicken Broth
- 1 Tbsp. Crushed Red Pepper

INSTRUCTIONS:

1. Bake chicken in a covered dish on 375°F until done.
2. Cool and pull apart to shred.
3. Add corn, green beans, diced tomatoes with chilis, Rotell, chicken broth, & crushed red peppers in a crock pot on high.
4. Add shredded chicken when done and cook on high for 3 hours.
5. Serve with tortilla chips and shredded cheese.

ESCAPE

by Becky

The majority of calls we received in my dispatch center were non-emergency calls. We took an abundance of alarm calls, barking dogs, someone asking for directions, civil disputes, and of course, several butt dialers. They came in sporadically throughout a shift. They were easy and quick to deal with. For new dispatchers, these calls were great to start with to get used to typing calls into the CAD and to gain the confidence that they could do it. They came a dime a dozen.

While working one evening, I already answered a few non-emergency calls with ease. Pretty straightforward – quick and easy. Without warning and out of nowhere, every phone line lit up. The non-emergency lines, as well as the 911 lines. It became noisy from all the ringing and my nerves tensed up. I sat straight up in my chair and was ready for whatever awaited on the other end of the line. My co-workers and I all took a nanosecond to look at each other in silence and knew it was game on. The look on our faces said it all - we are a team, and no matter what - we got this!

The first line I answered was someone telling me there was someone running across the road. My first thought was why is this an emergency. Then she told me he was wearing an orange jumpsuit that said "inmate" on the back of it, and then gave me a location that happened to be directly across the street from our county jail. I could see some of my co-workers were starting to enter calls into the CAD and realized what we were dealing with – someone escaped from jail. As we continued to take calls and get information, we quickly learned it wasn't just one inmate, but two inmates. I knew right away this wasn't going to be one of those easy calls. I knew I had to stay attuned to everything I was being told and quickly relay that information to the responding officers. Every call we took was like a missing piece of the puzzle or like breadcrumbs leading us to the inmates.

Citizens were quick to call in with every step the inmates took or every place they tried to hide. We tracked them across the street, in an apartment community close by, in sheds, knocking on doors, or just running down the street. They ditched their orange jumpsuits to try and blend in and did the best they could to getaway. They were in a fight or flight stage, but we never gave up. I remember taking one call after another. Getting more and more information to pass on or helping my co-workers dispatch information out over the radio. I'm not sure how much time elapsed before they were able to locate them and mark them in custody, but in the end, we did it. We all worked together as a team and were able to call it a success.

We learned it was two juveniles from our juvenile detention center. A short-term confinement facility used to house juveniles after they have been arrested but prior to their court date.

The juveniles were able to breach a secure area and beat two correction officers almost to death prior to their escape. They were left there to die, and one almost did. We were quick to send them medical attention and extra staff to re-secure the building. I remember seeing pictures of the area it took place in. Stuff was thrown around, and there was a lot of blood. My heart was broken for the correction officers involved and I prayed they would make a full recovery. I don't think one ever physically recovered and years later passed away. I was told the other one never emotionally recovered and never worked as a corrections officer again. I have a son that is a corrections officer today and have shared this story with him in hopes he never gets too comfortable and never lets his guard down – NEVER!

CHILD IN DANGER

by Becky

It's heartbreaking when you take a call involving a child. Even if you're not a parent, when children are involved, it tugs at your heart a little harder. I can remember a call that I knew would never make sense to me. No matter how hard I tried, I knew I would never understand how or why it happened or how to stop it.

I answered a 911 call from a young male, 12-13 years old, who was screaming for help. I knew it was bad when I first picked up the phone. The hair on the back of my neck immediately stood up from the panic in the voice on the other end of the line. He wanted someone to help his younger brother, who was five years old. He went on to tell me that his dad was very angry. He was yelling and screaming at both of them. He wasn't sure why he was so mad but then said he was talking to mommy on the phone right before he became angry. The boy then told me his dad had a knife. He was also holding on to his younger brother and threatening to stab him. Nothing the boy said to his father would calm him down. He was terrified! I could hear his dad yelling in the background, but I wasn't focused on him. I was concentrating on the boy. I listened very carefully to everything he told me - I was concerned about keeping him safe and trying to get help there as fast as I could to keep his brother safe too.

I asked the boy if he could get out of the house – he said no. He explained that his dad was in the front room by the door, and he was too scared to go near him. I instructed him to find another room in the house he could go to, shut the door and lock it. He was reluctant to leave his brother; he knew he was in danger, and he couldn't bring himself to leave that room. I explained to him I had several officers on the way to help his brother, and they were all coming very fast. I also explained to him that he needed to find a safe place for himself until this was over. I begged him first to save himself and hide from his dad – I begged him over and over to go to another room and lock himself in it. When things started to escalate with dad, he ran. He explained what room he was in, he locked the door, and then told me exactly where he was hiding. I stayed on the phone with him, and I could still hear the yelling in the background – not as good – but it was still there.

A very short time later, the police arrived. I knew they couldn't just barge inside and make everything better; they had to think about the safety of everyone – even dad. The police could hear dad yelling, and by this time, they could also see him. They could see how irate he was, the anger in his eyes, the child he clutched closely to him, and the knife. They tried to talk to him – they tried to calm him down – they tried everything, but he wasn't listening, and then it happened. They watched him stab his own son on the top of his head. At that moment, the officers had no choice but to rush in and save that child. They were able to get the child away from dad and then restrain him from harming anyone else or himself.

On these types of calls, we always start the medics in case things go south and are needed to provide immediate care. Most of the time, they aren't needed, but in this case, they were. Once the scene was secure, they rushed in to provide aid to the child and rushed him to the hospital.

I was still on the phone with the older boy who was in hiding. I stayed on the phone with him to be his safety net. I wanted to make sure he stayed in hiding, and he wanted to know what was going on in the living room. We were there for each other. After the events unfolded, I gave him very little information about what happened. I told him to stay put until an officer came and got him. They had to be the ones to explain what happened - they had to be the ones to endure his pain with him - they had to be the ones to see the horror unfold with one child and then comfort the tears of another.

Later that day, I was told the young boy would survive. I also found out that dad was so mad at mom he hurt their child to hurt her. I pushed this call in the back of my memory because I couldn't make sense of it; I didn't want to make sense of it. As a parent myself, I knew if I left the memories there, I would dwell on it. It would eat away at me day after day after day, and I would never be the same. It's calls like this that make dispatching hard, but saving a life makes it worth it!

BABY LOCKED IN CAR

by Becky

"9-1-1, what's the address of your emergency?" I started this call as any other emergency call.

"We are outside at the mall and there is a baby locked inside the car," the concerned caller told me.

"What's the phone number you're calling me from?" I replied.

"Did you hear me? There's a baby locked inside a car, and she's drenched with sweat!"

"Yes ma'am, I heard you. What's the phone number you're calling me from, please?" I asked again.

To the caller this exchange sounds like I am being insensitive and getting unnecessary information, when in fact, this information could be critical if we get disconnected. I would then have an address to send help to and her phone number to call her back immediately. It is sometimes hard to get information from people in emergency situations, but if you use a calm tone and some compassion, it helps. This is a call I took in July. One of the hottest months of the year here in Indiana.

After getting the necessary information, where the emergency was and her call back number, I immediately started the police and EMS (Emergency Medical Services) to her location. The police were on their way to help the child out of the car and then look for the person responsible for this. EMS was sent because the caller had already told me that the baby was drenched with sweat, so depending on how much time had passed she would most likely need medical care immediately.

"Ok, have you tried to open all of the doors on the car?" I asked.

"Yes, I have already checked them."

"Go ahead and check them again, right now," I directed. I could hear her trying to open the doors, and then she said that none of the doors would open.

"Is the baby crying?" I replied.

"No, she looks like she is asleep."

"Can you tell if she's breathing?"

"Yes, she is breathing. I can definitely tell she's still breathing. Labored breathing, but yes, she is still breathing."

"Knock on the window and see if you can get her to respond to you," I told her.

I heard a loud knock on the window through the phone, and then she indicated that there was no response from the baby. At this point I really wanted to tell her to break the window, but I couldn't. There are liabilities we face as 911 dispatchers that could bring lawsuits against our center, or even worse, against us. I knew I couldn't tell her to break the window when I wasn't there to actually see the situation firsthand, but I could tell her to take whatever means she thought necessary to get that child out - and I did. I could hear her in the background: asking for help from people nearby to go and try to find the owner of the vehicle, continuing to pound on the window in hopes she could set off an alarm, and trying the doors for the third time. I could hear the concern and desperation in her voice, and I kept telling her to do whatever she thought necessary at that moment to get that child out.

The police arrived on scene a few short minutes later, took one look at the baby and broke the window to get her out. The caller already told me that the baby had been in the car approximately 20 minutes prior to her call, and we were on the phone about 3-5 minutes before police arrived, so the total time that elapsed was at least 25 minutes that we knew of. It was documented to have been about 90 degrees that day, and they could tell the baby was definitely in distress. EMS was treating the baby and getting ready to transport her when the mother finally came out from her shopping spree.

My emotions were like a roller coaster on this call. I was first very worried about the welfare of the baby and wanted to get her out of the car immediately. I then became very angry at whoever would allow this to happen. How could anyone leave an infant in a locked car on a very hot day while they went shopping? After they got the baby out and she was being treated, I felt relieved that she was finally getting the help she so desperately needed. I was later told that she would be alright, and at that moment I knew I had another successful day in dispatch. I saved a life!

CHOCOLATE CHIP COOKIES

by Becky

I love to bake and made a lot of sweets for my coworkers. Baking is a stress reliever for me so I did it often. These were a favorite in the dispatch center. I was asked to make them again and again.

Prep Time: **20 min.** | *Cook Time:* **30 min.** | *Oven Temp:* **375°F**

INGREDIENTS

- ¾ c. Butter flavored Crisco
- 1 Egg
- 1 ¼ c. Light Brown Sugar
- 2 Tbsp. Milk
- 1 Tbsp. Vanilla Extract
- 2 c. Flour
- 1 tsp. Salt
- ¾ tsp. Baking Soda
- 1 sm. bag Semi-Sweet Chocolate Chips

INSTRUCTIONS:

1. Preheat oven to 375°.
2. Mix butter flavored Crisco, light brown sugar, milk, & vanilla in a large mixing bowl until creamy. Blend in egg.
3. In a separate bowl mix flour, salt, & baking soda.
4. Add to creamed mixture gradually until all mixed in.
5. Fold in chocolate chips.
6. Line a cookie sheet with parchment paper, With a cookie scoop drop rounded balls 3 inches apart on cookie sheet.
7. Bake 7 minutes - take out of oven and let them cool for 1-2 minutes. They will not look done but will continue to cook while cooling.
8. Place on a cooling rack.
9. Continue to bake dough until all cookies are done.
10. Makes 2 dozen. Store leftovers in an airtight container.

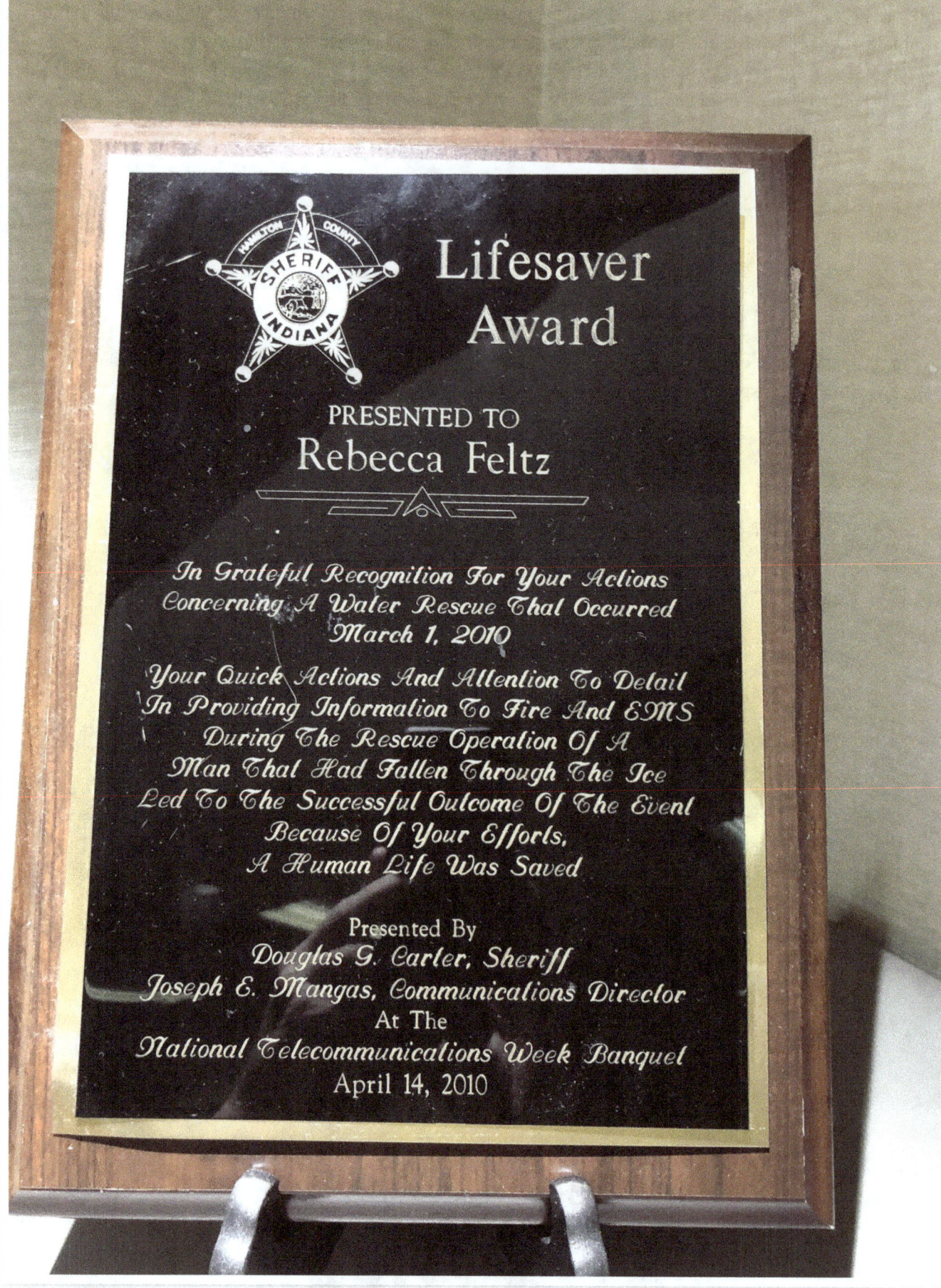

LIFESAVER AWARD

by Becky

In 2010 I was presented with the Lifesaver Award. I was recognized for my quick actions and attention to detail in providing information to fire and EMS during the rescue operation of a man that had fallen through the ice. My actions led to a successful outcome, and because of my efforts a humane life was saved!

March 1, 2010 began as any normal day for me. I woke up at 3:45 am, got ready for work, and clocked in at 4:55 a.m. I always drink coffee in the mornings, so I assume I already had a cup and was working on my second one. It was early, around 7:00 a.m., when I answered a 911 call.

The woman on the other end told me she thought there was an emergency somewhere nearby. She didn't have an exact address to give me, just her home address, but she could hear someone yelling for help. If I listened really hard there were times I could hear it in the background, too: "Help! Help me!" In Indiana at that time of year it is not quite daylight out, and it was a cold morning, so I knew I had a challenge ahead of me. The caller couldn't see anyone in the dark that needed help; she wasn't even sure which direction the cries were coming from. I immediately pulled up a map of the area to see what was around her house. I started asking questions like:

"Can you walk down the street and see anything?"

"Is there anyone else outside you can ask to help you?"

Her answer was always no. So I reassured her that the police were already dispatched to her home address to help. She continued to listen and tried to follow the voice in different directions. Still she came up short each time. At some point during the call I noticed that she lived somewhat near a lake, Geist Reservoir. It is a big lake that is used in the summer months for boating, skiing, fishing, and just relaxing. I asked her if she thought the cries could be coming from the lake area. I remember her being unsure because she thought they sounded too far away. I convinced her to walk toward the lake anyway and just check it out. The closer she got, the louder the voice got. So she kept going. She was as determined as I was to find this person! And that's when I heard her say, "I think there's someone in the lake."

By then the police were in the area, and they confirmed that yes, there was in fact a man in the water. I started EMS and a full water rescue. My teammates were also involved in accomplishing these important tasks. It was cold outside, and we all knew that we had to get this man out of the water quickly. I was still on the phone with the caller, and I could definitely hear the man in the background yelling for help. I explained to her that I had several people on the way and stayed on the line with her until an officer was right there with her. Then we disconnected. But the emergency was still not over, and the rest of the responders took over from there.

As dispatchers, we are responsible for answering the emergency calls, sending the appropriate people to help, and also documenting everything they tell us pertaining to that call. Documentation is important to keep track of where everyone is, to keep a time frame of events that happen, and to tell a story from start to finish. We are always there to call for additional help, if needed, and for anything else the responding units might need. We are all a team and work together to achieve success. I am not sure how long it took the rest of the team to get the man out of the water, but with the help of what seemed like an army, WE DID IT!

I learned later that this man we all helped save was ice fishing. He went out very early in the morning, cut a hole in the ice, and started fishing. This was a hobby, he explained, that he had done many, many times before. He enjoyed it and had never encountered a problem. It was March and quite cold outside, but we had a few warm days that must have thawed out the lake just enough to cave in with a little bit of weight and pressure. I'm not sure if he will continue to go ice fishing, and I'm not even sure he caught anything that day - except for a cold.

FISHBOWL GUY

by Becky

Not all calls we received in my dispatch center would require a police or fire response to be sent. We took calls from people asking for directions or needed a phone number for a local business. People would call to ask for advice on personal matters, and at times elderly people would call just to talk to someone. Then there were a select few that would call as a joke, and we would struggle to try and figure out how to react or respond to those calls. I remember one, in particular, we named "fishbowl guy."

I believe the first call came in as a non-emergency call. I wasn't the call taker on this one, but I later had my chance to talk to him – several of us did. When he called, he told the call taker he was watching his mom's house while she was out of town on vacation - not uncommon for people to do.

He also told us that his mom had a fishbowl with a goldfish in it. He really wanted to get a better look at it, so he stuck his head in the bowl - I'm sure the call taker was thinking he was crazy about now because why would anyone do that - but she kept going.

Next, he told her the bowl was stuck on his head – she's starting to think this is it. This is the real emergency. We are really going to send someone to get a fishbowl off of this guy's head. – Nope, his "real" emergency was he accidentally swallowed the fish. – silence from the call taker because she's not sure how to respond to that. "Fishbowl guy," said he swallowed the fish, and it was tickling his tummy; he even giggled like he was being tickled.

By this time, the call taker knew he really didn't have a true emergency, but she treated it as one and started asking the basic questions; what's your call back number, and what's the address of the emergency. Fishbowl guy kept talking about the fish in his belly and how it was swimming around and kept tickling him. (giggle - giggle) He was trying to get a reaction from the call taker, but she stayed professional, and he finally hung up. We all talked about the call, laughed about it, and thought we would never hear from him again……but we did.

"Fishbowl guy" called again several weeks later to say the fish was still in his belly tickling him and he wanted to know how to get it out. – The call taker this time didn't know anything about him, so he repeated his story about how it got there and then asked what he should do to get it out. She started to ask him the basic dispatch questions – and again - he hung up.

A couple of months had passed and to our surprise, "fishbowl guy" called again. This time I was the one to talk to him and was familiar with his ridiculous story. He explained his story again and then giggled and said the fish was still tickling his tummy. He asked again how he should get the fish out. – I decided to engage in conversation with him about the fish and was open to discussion on how to get the fish out. After all, I believe this was all "fishbowl guy" really wanted - someone to talk to. Even though I knew he wasn't serious, I couldn't even come up with any suggestions, but he did. He asked if he should swallow a fish hook to try and catch it. – At this point, I couldn't do anything but giggle with him. We chatted about the fish and then when I asked for his call back number and address – once again, for the third time he hung up!

It is often said that 911 dispatchers live in a fishbowl. We are faced with making difficult decisions, with incomplete or very little information under certain time restraints in an effort to fulfill our mission "to send the right people, at the right time, to the right location." While there is no way to get it correctly every single time, I would say collectively we have about a 90% success rate.

I'm not sure if "fishbowl" guy" was trying to bring light and amusement to our fishbowl, but non the less, we all listened to his absurd comical calls and still laugh about it today.

CROCK POT CHICKEN NOODLE SOUP

by Becky

Prep Time: **45 min.** | Cook Time: **5 hrs.** | Oven Temp: **Crockpot**

INGREDIENTS

3 lg. Chicken Breast, Cooked & Cubed

5 c. Chicken Broth

2 Tbsp. Butter

½ c. Onion

½ c. Carrots

½ c. Celery

1 can Corn, Drained

2 cans Cream of Chicken Soup

¼ c. Evaporated Milk

8 oz. Amish Egg Noodles, Essenhaus

Salt and Pepper to taste

INSTRUCTIONS:

1. Melt butter in a skillet - add onion, carrots, and celery to saute for about 4-5 minutes or until soft.
2. In a crock pot combine chicken stock, cream of chicken soup & evaporated milk.
3. Whisk together.
4. Add cooked chicken, sauted vegetables and corn. Cook on high for 3.5 hours.
5. Add noodles, stir in and cook for another hour on low.
6. Serve

CHOCOLATE & PEANUT BUTTER RITZ COOKIES

by Becky

This is a great sweet and salty snack you can't resist. I made them for a lot of our dispatch pitch-ins. They were loved by all and even adopted the name "Hockey Pucks."

Prep Time: **20-25 min.**

INGREDIENTS

1 Box Ritz crackers

16 oz. Peanut Butter

1 pkg. White or Chocolate Almond Bark

INSTRUCTIONS:

1. Place a generous amount of peanut butter between two ritz crackers. *Continue this until you have used the whole box of ritz or until you have the desired amount of cookies needed. (do not use any broken ritz).*
2. Melt the almond bark in a microwave safe bowl in 30 second increments stirring in between until all melted and smooth. **DO NOT OVERHEAT**. Dip each cookie in the chocolate and then place flat on parchment paper to dry. Serve immediately or place in airtight container and store in refrigerator until ready to serve.

I GOT THAT

by Becky

The correct terminology for a dispatch center is called Public Safety Answering Point or simply PSAP. A PSAP is responsible for answering emergency and non-emergency calls that are then sent to police, fire, or emergency services. A PSAP is staffed 24 hours a day, seven days a week, with trained professionals.

The PSAP I worked in was pretty small when I started, with only a maximum staffing of 5 and a minimum of 3 in the middle of the night. Over time and after we went through a consolidation, our center grew considerably. When I left, they occupied a new dispatch area that was equipped to staff 18 trained individuals at one time. Of course, the maximum and minimum numbers changed, but they never required all of those stations to be filled at once.

At times we would get calls from area hospitals advising they would be going on or off a diversion. There would be a need for hospitals to do this for hours or sometimes days. A diversion is when a hospital will request that ambulance patients be transported to another hospital. It doesn't mean the hospital is closed; it just means they are unable to treat any more additional patients without compromising the life of another patient already in their care.

One of those diversion calls sticks out in my head more than others. A co-worker that was sitting next to me answered the phone, and after a minute of listening, I heard her say "OK." There was another pause, and then she said, "Ok, I got it." She still wasn't able to hang up, so she continued to listen, and I heard again "I got that", and then again "I got that," and then yet again even louder, "I SAID I GOT THAT!" After then FINALLY, she was able to hang up.

I sat there listening to all of that and couldn't help but laugh and had to ask what all of that was about. She told me it was the hospital calling to say they were on diversion. She said the lady kept on talking and talking - Repeating herself over and over. We both laughed together, talking about what just happened, and then in fun and frustration, she said, "that bit@h just wouldn't shut up".

It was the little things like this that we would laugh about - a lot. After talking about it between the two of us and eventually a few others, we determined it was a recording. They knew the questions they would be asked and paused at just the right times and just long enough to make it appear it was a live person. – So, of course, we laughed even harder.

ATTEMPTED SUICIDE

by Becky

The number of successful suicides has increased over the years, and the age of those doing it are getting younger and younger. According to the CDC, in 2019, suicide deaths have claimed the lives of 47,500 people between the ages of 10 - 44. With the numbers growing every year for those that want to harm themselves, I'm not surprised by the number of calls we received at my 911 center. I've talked to a few people that wanted to harm themselves but remember one in particular. I spent an hour on the phone with her until we were able to locate her whereabouts to provide her with the help she needed.

When I first spoke to her, she wasn't clear about what she wanted. She told me she was having problems with her mom, at work, and her boyfriend. She talked about how her mom didn't like the things she did – she really didn't go into detail, just that her mom was upset with her. She talked about losing her job and then finally that her boyfriend broke up with her. I could tell in her voice that she was depressed - she just named several reasons why anyone would be - and then it dawned on me. She was calling for help because maybe she was having suicidal thoughts. As a 911 dispatcher, we've been trained to ask a few questions regarding this topic, but I wasn't sure if I should come right out and ask her – and then she said it, "I just want to kill myself."

I tried again to get her address to send help, but she wouldn't give it to me. She also wouldn't give me her phone number, but I already had it on my Ani/Ali screen; unfortunately, her cell phone only provided the address of the nearest cell tower. I decided to talk to her for awhile to build some type of connection with her. We talked about her family, other family members besides her mom. She had siblings and a father who loved her. I explained that things with her mom would change because a mother's love is unconditional. We talked about losing her job and how there would be other jobs out there. She was young and had her whole life ahead of her. Then we talked about her boyfriend. I think she was most upset about him. I remember talking at great lengths about him. I'm not a therapist – at least not a trained certified one- but I was able to talk to her about the good and bad memories she had with him. We talked about how things could change with him over time…… we just talked.

During our conversation, I was researching to try and get her address. My co-workers were there to help me along the way. When we talked about her family, I was able to get some names. I would write them down and hand them to someone to see if they could find a phone number or address. When we talked about her job, she mentioned what she did, not where she worked, but we had a starting point. My co-workers again made some calls to see if we could find her ex-employer. She definitely mentioned her boyfriend's name, but again we came up empty-handed. I remembered she told me she lived in an apartment and then mentioned she was out in her garage with her garage door open. I used the Ani/Ali tower address and knew she had to be somewhere within a 5-mile radius of that tower address. I gave all of the information I was able to get to the responding officers, and they started at the apartment complex they thought she was at and went door to door and rang doorbells. We were hoping she would have a reaction if her doorbell rang, or I would hear it through the phone. It worked – I heard it, and she definitely reacted to it.

I relayed the information to the officers when they were at the correct address, but she would not answer the door. She was getting angry, and the sound of the doorbell was upsetting her - in a bad way. She kept telling me to make them stop, or she was just going to kill herself - right then – right now! This went on for several minutes, and they kept ringing the doorbell – over and over. She was sick of hearing it and decided to go back out into the garage. When she told me that, I knew we had our way in – I remembered the garage door was opened. They finally made contact with her and took her to get the professional help she needed. Over an hour on the phone – my job was over.

Talking to someone threatening suicide isn't something anyone should take lightly, that is why I spent more than an hour on the phone with her that day. Also, as a dispatcher, you have to balance empathy with detachment to provide yourself with some safety. You can't take these things personally or hold onto them, or they will ruin your career or, worse – your life. That day I was able to help her choose life over death at that moment and I hope she chose life every day after that.

DISPATCHER BIO

Lisa Jeffries. I was born and raised in the small town of Atlanta, Indiana. People often mistake it for Georgia, but it is indeed much smaller (population 1,000 or less). There were three kids in my family: my older brother Ray and my younger brother Bob. And I was the adorable middle child - or so I thought. I grew up in the '60s and '70s - a time when things were much simpler and the music was much better.

My Dad was a GM factory worker, and my Mom was a stay-at-home mom. I attended the Hamilton Heights school system, where I made some really good friends. Most are still close to me today, which I attribute to the small town mentality. My parents owned and operated a small restaurant in their time off when I was young, so my older brother and I would help out from time to time. It was a very popular place, and local folks loved to come and enjoy the food.

When I turned 14 or 15, I started working part time at the local grocery store as a cashier during the summer and in the evenings after school. There were many times I would be required to lock up at night or open up in the mornings, taking the store key home with me. I really didn't think anything about it at the time, but looking back on it now, I think, "Who gives a 14 or 15 year old that kind of responsibility?" It's pretty mind blowing, since I was not even old enough to drive to and from work. While working at the store I met my husband, Bob, and at the time he had just accepted the position of town marshal. We dated awhile and were engaged when I was 16 (crazy, I know!) and then married my senior year (1977), when I was 17. I took a job at a local shoe store, where I worked full time and finished out my senior year. I am sure kids these days think this is totally insane. I know my three kids do! But it was a sign of the times, I think, and it all worked out fine.

My husband Bob took a position at the Noblesville Police Department as a patrolman, and our first son was born in 1980. I worked at the shoe store for five years, and then I applied at the Hamilton County Sheriff's Department as a Dispatcher. I started there in 1982 and worked as a dispatcher for two years and was then promoted to Supervisor, which involved dispatching and supervising. Our department was very small back then and pretty close-knit; they were like my second family.

When I first started, we worked with two dispatchers on a shift and only dispatched police for the county and the smaller towns (Arcadia, Fishers, Cicero, Sherdian, Atlanta). Noblesville Police and Carmel Police had their own dispatch centers. Our dispatch center was located in the heart of the "old" jail, so we actually had to multitask and operate the jail doors and garage overhead doors, as well as monitor the various cameras throughout the building and an alarm panel for the various banks . This could be a very daunting task if we were busy with hot calls and emergency radio traffic.

One of our beloved correctional officers was very handy and fashioned us a stick with rubber bands on one end to help reach the door controls when we were busy, as well as a plastic cover for the alarms (that were audible and rang very loud in the room) that could not be silenced. Also, at the time, the jail did not always have a female officer to book in and pass meds and such to the female inmates, so the dispatchers had to do this job, too, which could be very interesting. Ah, the good old days! I cannot remember the exact date we started dispatching for the fire department, but the tiny console we used for it was hilarious when compared to today's standards. But then again, our dispatching with a boom mic was also standard for the time.

In 1984, our second son was born, and in 1991, our daughter was born. There were lots of changes taking place between those years and one of our new dispatch centers was built. I remember giving tours of the new center when our daughter was only one year old. When she was about 18 months old, I went to college at IUK (Kokomo) during my time off. This was a fun but very stressful time for me, often going to class until 11 p.m. and getting up at 4 a.m. to go to work. At the time I thought I wanted to go into nursing but later changed my mind when it came time for my clinicals.

911 Emergency Dispatchers, Public Safety Responders | 51

In 2014, after 32 years in dispatch (later re-named Communications), I retired. It was bittersweet for me. The job I had once loved had become extremely stressful and not a very healthy environment for me. I was sad to not see the people I had worked so closely with for years and had developed close friendships with on a daily basis. But I was happy to not have the stress that always surrounded me, even on my days off.

In 2015, I started a new job as a part-time visitation clerk in our jail. It was almost like coming back home, but without all the stress and hectic atmosphere. In 2016, I was offered a full-time position in the jail in the same role, and that was a very positive move for me. I am still somewhat in touch with those in Communications, as well as new work friends in the jail.

In April, 2021, our daughter made us grandparents for the first time with a little girl. This has opened a whole new chapter of our lives! Our hobbies have always been travel, fishing, and antiquing, just to name a few, so we plan to do so many fun things in the years to come with the family.

LISA'S POWDER SUGAR COOKIES

by Lisa

My favorite shapes are Stars, Bells, and Christmas trees.

Prep Time: **20 min.** | Cook Time: **30 min.** | Oven Temp: **375°F**

INGREDIENTS

1 ½ c. Powder Sugar

1 c. Butter, softened

1 Egg

1 tsp. Vanilla

2 ½ c. Flour

1 tsp. Cream of Tartar

1 tsp. Baking Soda

1 tsp. Almond Extract

INSTRUCTIONS:

1. Mix softened butter, powdered sugar, egg, vanilla and almond extract together.
2. Sift flour, cream of tartar and baking soda in a mixing bowl.
3. Gradually mix flour mixture to Powdered Sugar mixture and blend well.
4. Roll out the cookie dough on a floured surface, and cut out your desired designs.
5. Bake on 350 for 10 minutes until lightly browned.

MULTI-CAR PILE UP

by Lisa

When you work in a 911 dispatch center, the call volume typically changes throughout the day. Sometimes, the day will start off with a bang - busy with radio traffic and calls. Other times the day starts off slowly and then ends with a bang, but there is never a dull moment. The morning of February 3, 2009, was no exception and turned out to be one of those days that started with a bang and then just stayed that way all day!

The forecast for weather that day was "a light dusting of snow," according to the local news station. Those became haunting words as the phones soon began to ring, one right after another, and radio traffic was nonstop with reports of a multi-car pile-up on I-69 in the Fishers area. The calls reported semi trailers, cars, and trucks involved, with serious injuries. I was the working supervisor that day and ended up going in to help answer calls and give breaks to those working the incident. This became a multi-agency detail where many neighboring agencies came to assist with traffic and whatever was needed.

As always, in any police/fire incident, the officers involved as well as the callers are monitored and given instructions to curtail further injuries on the accident scene. The reports I received listed anywhere from 22-32 vehicles involved, so the responders had their hands full and we also received dozens and dozens of 911 calls. There were calls from people who ran off the road to avoid the crash, those actually involved, and those drivers passing by and witnessing it all unfold. State highway patrol, multiple wrecker services, additional medics, fire apparatus, and portable toilets were all brought out. To say it was a huge incident is an understatement; it even made the national news and was all people could talk about for quite awhile.

There was one call I can still remember that was taken by another dispatcher next to me. The caller was a female trapped in her vehicle. We were accustomed to getting calls from entrapped people involved in accidents, but this caller was trapped under a semi truck. The woman was hysterical, and I just remember the calming effect that the dispatcher had during the call, staying on the line until the emergency responders arrived to assist her. There were several calls very similar to this one where people were involved and upset or injured. Unfortunately, with this severe incident, there was loss of lives as well.

I was never more proud of our dispatch center and the professionalism shown to all involved. In the midst of chaos there was compassion, organization, and a group of dispatchers working together with a common goal to quickly and efficiently send help to those in need. I was never more pleased and honored to be a part of such a professional and unique organization.

** There was a huge "white" dry erase board in our old center at the time of this incident. It was used primarily for informational purposes, such as units working in which area of the county, town officers, or other information to be passed on shift to shift. During this incident, it was used as a stress relief drawing board**

Over 40 car pile up on interstate. The white board was used to give us an overview of how many response apparatus were involved

FUDGE

by Lisa

Don't be fooled, this is extremely easy but very tasty and satisfies your sweet tooth. This was made many times at dispatch and by the end of the shift it was gone.

Prep Time: **5 min.** | Cook Time: **7 min.**

INGREDIENTS

2 c. Sugar
½ c. Milk
3 Tbsp. Peanut Butter
½ tsp. Vanilla

INSTRUCTIONS:

1. In a medium sized saucepan, add all ingredients and mix together.
2. Cook over medium heat, stir until smooth.
3. Once the mixture begins to rapidly boil, stir the mixture constantly for 5 minutes.
4. Remove from the heat and stir an additional 2 minutes, it will begin to dull slightly.
5. Pour into a glass, buttered pie plate. Let cool completely

Slice & Serve. Enjoy!

TRAINING CLASSES

by Lisa

During the time I worked in dispatch, I was very fortunate to be sent to a variety of training classes for police and fire incidents. One in particular that stands out was hosted by the local fire department and involved active participation in an active house burn. The fire department had a house staged with accelerants that would burn the house in stages and would demonstrate the extent of the fire damage and the speed that it can occur in the right conditions. The first thing we did was become familiar with all the equipment used and were shown how to operate it. Handling the fire hose was certainly the most challenging. It's even more powerful than I imagined! Along with the smaller equipment we became familiar with, we also were shown the various fire apparatuses used in different types of fires.

We were also outfitted in the turn-out gear (the uniforms that firefighters wear) in order to enter the house and witness the engulfment. Well, I wore everything except for the helmet (SCBA) because it completely covers the face, and it was too claustrophobic for me! Putting on the uniform and then actually entering a building in flames gave so much appreciation for what our firefighters do every day.

This training has always stood out for me because it showed the danger and complexity of dealing with these unpredictable situations and how the entire dynamic of the scene can change rapidly. I realized how easy it is to take for granted what our firefighters and police officers do for us and our communities, and I wish everyone would have a chance to experience this kind of training so they could be more grateful to our first responders.

OLD FASHIONED BISCUITS

by Lisa

Prep Time: **10 min.** | *Cook Time:* **25 min.** | *Oven Temp:* **450° F**

INGREDIENTS

2 c. Self-Rising Flour

¼ tsp. Baking Soda

1 ¼ tsp. Salt

6 Tbsp. Lard

1 c. Buttermilk

Melted Butter to taste

INSTRUCTIONS:

1. Whisk together the dry ingredients, (flour, baking soda, salt) in a large bowl till combined.
2. Add the cold lard to dry ingredients and cut it into the flour, using a pastry cutter or a fork, until it resembles coarse meal.
3. Add the cold buttermilk into the bowl and stir with a spoon or a rubber spatula, JUST until combined. This only should take a few stirs. The dough will be pretty wet and sticky at this point.
4. Turn dough out onto a lightly floured work surface. With floured hands, gently pat out (do NOT roll with a rolling pin) the dough until it's about ½ inch thick.
5. Fold the dough in half and then turn it 90 degrees. Pat it out and fold it again. Do this process about 6 times
6. Preheat oven to 450 degrees.
7. Bake for 12- 15 minutes till golden brown.

Do not open the oven door for AT LEAST the first half of baking time. You want the steam to stay trapped in the oven, helps them to rise. For a smaller biscuit, you may not need to bake as long.

Brush biscuits with melted butter if desired.

ANGRY GEESE

by Lisa

I received a call from a utility worker during the day shift in the dispatch center. He was working on site with a meter and called urgently requesting police assistance. Unable to imagine why he could possibly need the police for his meter work, so I asked him what his emergency was. He told me that he was being attacked repeatedly by angry geese every time he got close to the meter. He had tried several times to complete his task, but the angry birds would not leave him alone and were becoming more and more hostile!

The caller was in the process of explaining this scenario and giving me his information and location when the phone went dead. I was a little concerned, but mostly curious how he was getting along with the geese. What could have happened?

A little while later he called back and apologized for dropping the call, but one of the geese had tossed his cell phone in the pond! The man took this all in good stride, considering he still had his job to do and the task was being delayed. I had to stifle my laughter until after we disconnected, and then I got a big kick out of what had happened. I have always wondered if he laughed when he shared this story in years to come, or if he was too embarrassed to tell how some geese got the better of him.

911 Emergency Dispatchers, Public Safety Responders

CIVIL WAR

by Lisa

The day shift at the dispatch center is fairly calm, compared to the evening shift - mostly vehicle VIN checks, accidents, and minor violations. On one particular day, in the late 1980s, I took a call about an accident involving damage to a mailbox out in the county area. I could tell that the owner of the mailbox in question was a very elderly gentleman, and the officer I sent out was one of the nicest guys we had in the department at the time. When he arrived on the scene, he made his incident report and took all the information from both parties. As we do frequently, even on less urgent calls, we tend to check on our officers when they are out on the scene for a long period of time without any communication. It had been several minutes since I had heard from the officer, so, according to procedure, I hit him on the air to check in - "Sig 45," as we called it. After a pause, he answered correctly and said he would be 10-6 ("busy") for awhile.

About an hour later, the officer marked "back in service," indicating that he was available for other calls. I thought that was an extreme amount of time for a minor accident involving just a mailbox, but I had to move on to other calls and responsibilities.

Towards the end of my shift, the officer came in and told me about what had happened. The old gentleman was quite a storyteller and had gotten on a roll sharing tales with the officer. During the course of the conversation, the officer offered to help the man with the repair of his mailbox. A quick job, he thought, and a kind gesture. But he soon realized that he had stumbled into more than he bargained for when the man took out his set of tools - all from the Civil War era! Even the nails that the officer had to use for the repair were badly rusted and crooked, apparently well used for years and years.

To his credit, he completed the repair, and we both had a good laugh about it. All in a day's work for an officer!

BACON CAULIFLOWER SALAD

by Lisa

This is a great salad for any picnic or family get together. I take this salad to many of the parties we attend.

Prep Time: **20 min.** + Chilling

INGREDIENTS

1 Med. Cauliflower, broken into florets
1 lb. Bacon, cooked and crumbled
1 c. Cheddar Cheese, cubed
1 Med. Green Pepper, chopped
1 Med. Onion, chopped
1 c. Mayonnaise
2-4 tsp Sugar
1 Head Broccoli

INSTRUCTIONS:

1. In a large mixing bowl, combine cauliflower, Broccoli, bacon, cheese, green pepper and onion,
2. In another bowl, combine mayonnaise, and sugar.
3. Spoon over cauliflower mixture and toss to coat.
4. Cover and refrigerate at least 4 hours.

INSTA POT SALSA CHICKEN

by Lisa

Prep Time: **10 min.** | Cook Time: **25 min.**

INGREDIENTS

- 1 ½ lbs. Chicken Breast, boneless and skinless
- 2 tsp. Chili Powder, Ancho or Regular
- 1 tsp. Ground Cumin
- 1 tsp. Ground Corriander
- Salt and Pepper to taste
- 1 clove Garlic
- 1 c. Salsa of choice
- 2 Tbsp. Cilantro, chopped
- 10 Tortilla shells
- Toppings of choice: Lettuce, Cheese, Tomatoes, Sour Cream etc

INSTRUCTIONS:

1. In a small bowl, whisk together chili powder, cumin, coriander and ¼ tsp pepper. Add more later if you think you will need it.
2. Sprinkle this dry mixture evenly over both sides of the chicken breast, sprinkle the minced garlic over the chicken, then pour salsa over the chicken to cover it.
3. Once you have your chicken breasts covered with all your ingredients: Close the lid, turn vent to " sealing" and set instant pot to poultry or manual, then set to 13 minutes.
4. If using a slow cooker, cook 5-6 hours on low heat.
5. After your chicken is done. Remove and let cool, several minutes, then shred and return to the juices in your slow cooker or instant pot.
6. Sprinkle in Cilantro and toss to coat.
7. Lift chicken pieces with tongs, or slotted spoon to allow excess liquid to run off.
8. Place in tortilla shells
9. Add your favorite toppings

Enjoy

PEEL AWAY THE POUNDS SOUP

by Lisa

This is an old WW recipe I tweaked some. You could really add more "free" vegetables of your liking, as long as you stayed within the core recipe

Prep Time: **15 min.** | Cook Time: **20 min.**

INGREDIENTS

- 1 head Cabbage, chopped
- 3 lg. Onions, chopped
- 3 stalks Celery, chopped
- 2 lg. Green Peppers, chopped
- 2 cans Tomatoes, chopped with liquid
- 1 tsp. Salt
- 1 tsp. Pepper
- Garlic Powder to taste

INSTRUCTIONS:

1. Place all ingredients in a large stock pot and cover with water.
2. Bring to a boil and then simmer until vegetables are tender, around 30 minutes. But the longer it simmers and " marries ", the better the flavor.

911 Emergency Dispatchers, Public Safety Responders

CONTEMPLATING SUICIDE

by Lisa

There is a story from my dispatching days that I end up telling quite a bit because it meant so much to me. Sometimes as dispatchers we have the chance to make a big difference in the outcome of an event or in someone's life, and those are the good moments we never forget.

I took a call from a male who was very upset and contemplating suicide. He was just driving around the county, going no place specific but planning his death. After a short time into the call, I realized that I was talking to my neighbor, so I identified myself. I wanted him to know that I cared and was more than just a voice on the phone. We talked for a long time while he drove around. Officers were attempting to locate him as well. At that time we did not have all the locating tools that are currently in place, but my neighbor was unintentionally very helpful with little hints he was giving me about his location.

He confided to me that he and his girlfriend had a huge fight, and he felt that suicide was the answer to his problems. I talked to him for a very long time and explained to him that his life was valuable, that so many people would miss him, and that he still had so many things in his life to look forward to. It was a very hard call because he was crying and so distraught, plus knowing him personally made it so much more difficult to stay calm on my end. Our conversation continued for some time and eventually he calmed down, met the officers searching for him, and talked to them for quite awhile. Before he hung up the phone, he thanked me for caring and being there for him. It was a moment that I will never forget.

The next day, when I was at home, I received a knock at my door. When I answered, it was my neighbor, wanting to thank me in person and give me flowers, not just him but from his girlfriend, too. I was deeply touched. I have had so many different calls in my career - some went well, others not very well. But this one will always hold a special place in my heart.

The National Suicide Prevention Lifeline is a national network of local crisis centers that provides free and confidential emotional support to people in suicidal crisis or emotional distress 24 hours a day, 7 days a week. We're committed to improving crisis services and advancing suicide prevention by empowering individuals, advancing professional best practices, and building awareness.

ABOUT THE LIFELINE   800-273-8255
www.suicidepreventionlifeline.org

SWEET POTATO SOUFFLE

by Lisa

Prep Time: **15 min.** | Cook Time: **40 min.** | Oven Temp: **350° F**

INGREDIENTS

- ½ c. Butter, room temperature
- ¾ c. Light Brown Sugar
- 3 c. Mashed Sweet Potatoes
- 2 lg. Eggs
- 1/3 c. Milk
- 2 tsp. Vanilla
- 1 tsp. Cinnamon
- ½ tsp. Salt
- 1 lb. Pecans, crushed

INSTRUCTIONS:

1. Mix together the butter, and brown sugar for about 1 minute, till combined. Add your sweet potatoes, eggs, milk, vanilla, cinnamon and salt. Continue mixing until very smooth, 1-2 minutes. Spread this mixture in your coated 2-quart baking dish.

2. TOPPING MIX; In a large bowl, combine 1C of copped pecans. 3/4C Light Brown Sugar, 1/2 C all-purpose flour, 1/4 cup butter at room temp. Spread topping on the sweet potato mixture.

3. Pre-Heat oven to 350. Coat a 2-quart baking dish with non-stick spray.

4. Bake for 40 minutes, until browned on top. The filling will be slightly jiggly.

5. Place the pecans on top and bake another 5 minutes. Allow Souffle' to cool for 10-15 minutes before serving.

This casserole can be prepped up to a day in advance, stored airtight in the refrigerator. When ready to bake, take out of fridge 15 mins before baking.

BACK YARD DEER

by Lisa

Being a 911 dispatcher not only takes quick thinking but also creative problem solving and patience. I once took a call from a concerned woman who lived within the city limits of our county and was troubled about a deer in her backyard. I could tell right away she was pretty worried.

When I asked her what exactly the problem was, she said, "This deer is clearly lost from its home in the woods! It's in my fenced-in backyard, and I'm just worried that it won't be able to get out and find the way back to its family!"

I didn't tell her that the deer would have no problem finding its way back over the fence and returning to its family. Instead, I asked, "Does your fence have a gate?"

"Yes, it does!" she replied.

"Well why don't you open the gate so the deer can find its way out," I suggested.

And she did. Sometimes it's easier to just solve problems that aren't really problems and do your best to make the public happy.

THEY KNOW ME

by Lisa

Some people say that dinosaurs still roam the earth during third shift from 10:00 p.m. to 6:00 a.m., and while I've never seen any dinosaurs, I can definitely say that weird things happen during those hours. Once, during the night shift, a 911 call came through on a violent domestic in Sheridan, a small town in our county. The caller was frantic on the other end of the line, yelling about a crazy man who was going nuts and acting very erratic. That particular area belonged that night to Officer P., a colorful officer whom I knew well. He responded with a "Signal 10," so I knew he was en route. Then I started thinking about my officer, as all dispatchers do. I knew he was responding to a possibly violent person, and I didn't know how safe he would be. Would he be able to gain control of the situation? I tried to get additional information from the caller, but that was not much help. I knew other officers were responding as backup, but they were still a good distance away. I was concerned.

As my officer arrived, he informed me that a number of other people were trying to help subdue the male subject who was causing the disturbance. After a while - what seemed like an eternity - the other officers arrived on the scene and aided Officer P. and the good Samaritans. Fortunately, the suspect was apprehended without any serious injuries to anyone. He was handcuffed and placed in Officer P.'s squad car. While en route to the jail, the detainee continued to remain violent - kicking, yelling, and bouncing around in the back seat. At this point, Officer P. stopped his car to reposition the detainee and confine him more securely. Without much success, though, because shortly the detainee managed to free his feet and kick officer P.'s back seat, causing his radio mic to stick open. Now the rest of the dispatchers and I could hear everything going on in the car.

We were all listening to the detainee's yelling and colorful language when very unexpectedly he said, " I know Bob and Lisa Jeffries!"

It took my brain a second to realize, that's me! The other dispatchers burst into laughter.

"Hey, Lisa, get your family under control!" they teased, even though I had no idea who this man was (and never did find out).

Finally, Officer P. arrived and delivered the detainee into the custody of the jailers. He came to the dispatch center later to tell me that I should have t-shirts made that say, "I know Bob and Lisa Jeffries." Apparently, this was the second individual that week who had told Officer P. that very same thing! More laughter from my fellow dispatchers, of course. Well, sometimes you can't help but be popular with the locals!

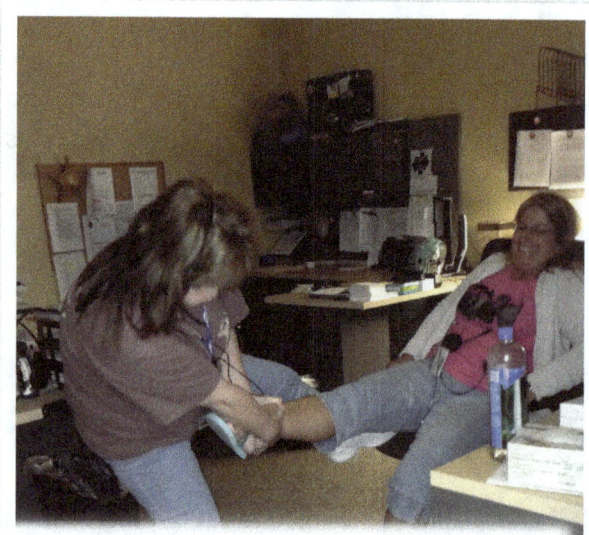

Lisa was having back pain that day. Missy (me) thinking I was a medical professional was trying to pull on her legs to unlock her back. That's what my chiropractor always did!

LISA LISA

by Lisa

I took a 911 call once from a woman who was concerned about her adult son and his behavior. She told me that he was bipolar, manic depressive, and a number of other concerning mental health issues. He was living with her and was off his medication. He had recently gone through a nasty break up with his wife, and the mere mention of her name was enough to set him off emotionally.

The mother called that day because her son was acting very oddly, and she was worried that he would go into a violent episode. While we were on the phone, the son picked up another phone in the house and was listening in on our conversation. Everything was going well until the end of the call when she asked my name.

"My name is Lisa," I told her.

"Oh no," she replied.

"Is there a problem?" I responded.

"That's the name of his ex-wife!" she exclaimed. "Please hurry!"

So I was there to help but ended up being a trigger without meaning to!

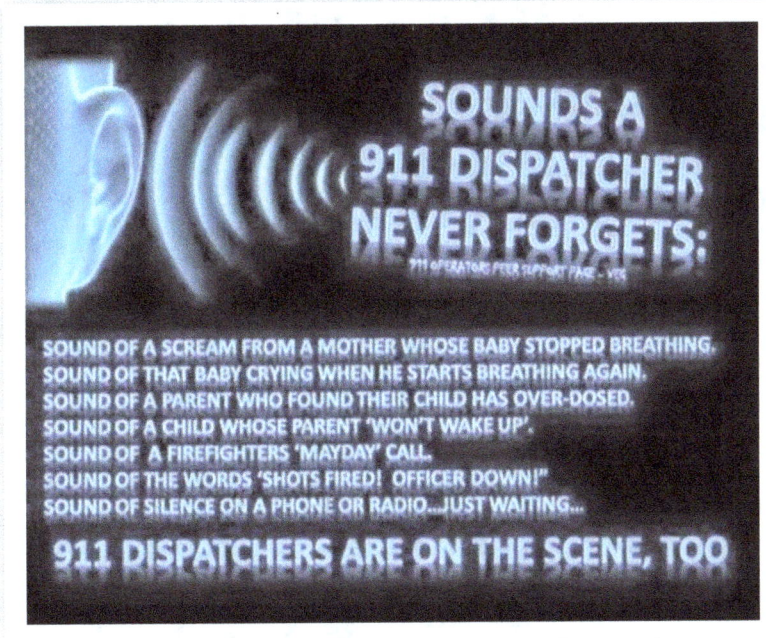

DISPATCHER BIO

Pam McGee-Higgs. I was born in Noblesville, Indiana, where I still reside. I graduated from Noblesville High School in 1978 and then attended and graduated from the Indiana Barber School Academy. I cut hair for a couple years but it was not for me, so I started working at a local peat bog plant. My job was watching a machine fill plastic bags with peat moss, and I even learned to drive a fork truck and a backhoe! When I turned 21, I started tending bar at a local club in the evening and babysitting during the day. One of the families I babysat for was the major at our local sheriff's department. He came home one day and asked if I wanted to be a dispatcher. I didn't even know what that was! But why not give it a shot? I thought. So I went in and filled out the application and was quickly interviewed and then hired. That was January, 1984, and I had just turned 24 years old.

The dispatch center was located inside our local jail. It included the sheriff, all the deputies, investigation division, jail deputies, dispatchers, kitchen staff, and prisoners. When I started working there as a dispatcher, we had no computers or headsets or anything like that. We typed our logs and wrote out " run cards " to keep track of our officers on calls. We kept our run cards in a slotted wooden square made by one of our maintenance staff, which was very handy. We also monitored the cameras, the jail building and grounds, and the padded cell. We opened and closed the doors inside the building too, all day long. We were quite talented - talking on the radio and taking an emergency call on a hand-held phone propped on our shoulder while opening the doors with a stick that looked like a pool stick, all at the same time! There were no female jail deputies at the time, so the dispatchers doubled as matrons. We patted down the female prisoners, booked them in jail, and at times even did body cavity searches (I hadn't signed up for that!). We passed their meals and their meds and generally took care of the female population at the jail.

Eventually it came time for computers and 911 lines. No one liked THE change, but it was inevitable. The first time the 911 line rang into our center, it was terrifying, even though we had taken the same calls on the seven digit lines just the day before. I remember that first call so well because no one wanted to answer it. I didn't either, but I took a deep breath and picked it up. It was an elderly man from a small town in our community who just wanted to know, " Do you know what the score of that thar football game was last night ? " Not so bad after all! Very soon, we loved the computers and headsets and new system. When it would malfunction or they would take it down for maintenance, we cringed. Then back we went to handwriting our run cards and had to get that wooden block out of hiding.

During my 31 years of dispatching, I helped deliver three babies - two at the homes of the mothers and one in the backseat of a deputy's squad car, during a snowstorm. I talked the deputy through the whole procedure, over the radio, from our protocol cards. He and I like to joke and say, "We had a baby together."

There are also many hard calls that we have to put out of our minds. I have three tragic incidents that I have carried in my heart for a very long time and still carry today. I think about those from time to time and wonder how the mother is doing after she lost her son in a fire, how the boy is that shot and killed his brother. That's the hard part of being a dispatcher: most of the time we don't get to know the ending of the situation. I was lucky enough to take only two calls involving a family member and a wonderful young man that I babysat for; neither call ended well, and I still have a heavy heart with those.

I remember that on September 11th I was taking a heart attack call over 911 when my dispatch partner motioned for me to look at the TV. I could not believe what I was seeing, but of course I could not stop taking the heart attack call. I also could not believe that our small sheriff's department, in central Indiana, had to guard and protect certain places that were located within our county.

In 2015, I retired from public safety dispatching after 31 years. I am now the Hamilton County Circuit Court Bailiff. I love this job. But if I'm being honest, I loved being a dispatcher the most. The friends, family, and memories I made during that time are so special. I will never forget that time or the people I worked with. I have treasured every minute of it. There are so many good memories that it would take an entire series of novels to share them all. I hope to retire for good very, very soon and move south to a warmer climate. I hope that in my career as a dispatcher I made a difference in someone's life and will be remembered fondly in our current center by the " old dawgs " still working there.

In my spare time, I have volunteered with a Cocker Spaniel rescue group. I have driven as far as Kentucky to pick up one dog, at a high kill shelter. He lived with me for 15 years and was the best dog. By working with this rescue group, I ended up with four cocker spaniels at one time! On a rainy, muddy day, just one step inside the house with the dogs meant 16 pawprints! But I wouldn't have it any other way. I love dogs - more than people most days - because no matter what breed, they give you unconditional love their entire lives. I used to volunteer at our local Humane Society, which was on the same property as our dispatch center. When I would leave work, I would go there and walk the dogs, feed them, play with them, and just love them. This brought me peace on those difficult days in dispatch. Knowing that I made a difference in their difficult days at the shelter, made mine a whole lot brighter!

I met the love of my life, Robert, in 2009. We finally married in Gatlinburg, Tennessee, in 2017. I was 57 years old before I made my first trip down the aisle. Oh how I wish my precious mother would have been alive to be there! But she was there in my heart. I have taken her recipes and will be sharing them in this book along with my stories. I hope you enjoy them!

SO, that's my story in a nutshell. Dispatch isn't for the faint of heart. It takes a very special person. I've had the privilege to work with them all. I thank them for being away from their families on all the major holidays, birthdays and just being away for hours at time. I was very blessed to have a job I absolutely loved for 31 years. Memories I will treasure for a lifetime.

TEESH'S CUCUMBER DIP

by Pam

During our pitch in's, this is the dip I would make for (Teesh) . It's really good with Chicken n Biscuit crackers Holy Cow Teesh !!!

Prep Time: **5 min.**

INGREDIENTS

1 lg. Cucumber

8 oz. Cream Cheese

Garlic Powder to taste

Season Salt to taste

INSTRUCTIONS:

1. Peel your cucumber. Remove the seeds, cut lengthwise and use a spoon to scrape out the seed.
2. Grate your entire cucumber.
3. Soften your cream cheese Add garlic powder, season salt Mix together.
4. Don't add anything, if you think it may be to thick. The cucumber has a lot of moisture, it will be fine.

PORK STEAK & POTATOES

by Pam

My Mother made this recipe up. My husband and I enjoy it still today. Of course, hers was better, but we certainly try. It really is a great dinner meal, serve with a side of fresh veggies, and maybe some roles.

Prep Time: **10 min.** | *Cook Time:* **2.5 hrs.**

INGREDIENTS

2 lg. Pork Steaks
1-2 Tbsp. Worcestershire Sauce
1-2 Tbsp. Soy Sauce
3 med-lg Red Potatoes
Season Salt to taste
Garlic Powder to taste
Black Pepper to taste

INSTRUCTIONS:

1. Brown pork steaks in a large skillet that has a lid. After browning, cover steaks in water.
2. Add Worcestershire Sauce Soy Sauce.
3. Cover and cook about 2 hours. Pork steaks will be very tender, remove the bone from the steaks.
4. When steaks are done. Slice your potatoes, to your desired thickness. Layer the potato's on top of your meat. You may have to add a little more water at this point. Don't stir. This is basically gong to steam your potato's
5. Cover Potato's with Season Salt, Garlic Powder, Black pepper.
6. Cover with your lid, and cook another 20 mins till potatoes are done.
7. Remove the lid, and continue cooking till the moisture is almost gone.

KIDNAPPED

by Pam

There was one time, Connie had a small plastic porky pig. She gave it to our Dispatch Captain at the time. It sat on his desk. I don't know whose idea this was, but it was a fun time had by all. We kidnapped that small plastic pig. And held him for ransom.

Someone had a camera that printed pictures on the spot. Our first ransom demand was for donuts. We took a picture of Porky blindfolded and a cutout newspaper letter ransom note. We got our donuts. Our 2nd demand was for Gas Station big gulp drinks. We took another picture of Porky, where we were going to hang him. And the magazine cut out letters for the ransom note. YEP, we got out Big Gulps. Our last ransom demand was for Dairy Queen. So, we thought this picture of Porky should be more dramatic. So, we recruited one of the Deputies to hold their Glock to Porky's head. And we sent our dairy queen demand. YES, we all got ice cream from Dairy Queen.

Connie passed away, and her friend Lu wanted me to have Porky; since THEY SAY (whoever that is), I was the kidnapping instigator. That plastic pig sits above my kitchen sink to this day, well over 30 years.

It still makes me smile with these silly things we got into back in the day. Harmless fun times.

SOUTHERN GREEN BEANS

by Pam

My Mother worked 3rd shift as long as I can remember. She would make these green beans for the entire week, for us to eat. She would cook the main course in the evening, but these were always a staple in our house. Mom and Dade always had a huge garden, mostly green beans and tomatoes. So these green beans were extra good from her canning jars.

Prep Time: **20 min.** | Cook Time: **2 hrs.**

INGREDIENTS

4 Slices Bacon / Jowl / Side meat
2 lbs. Green Beans, Frozen or Fresh
3 c. Chicken Broth
3 Tbsp. Butter

INSTRUCTIONS:

1. Fry your choice of the meat in a large pot. Remove the meat. Leave the drippings in the pan.
2. Add green beans to your Pot Cover your beans with the chicken broth.
3. Bring to a low boil, for 1 1/2 hours to 2 hours, stirring occassionally.
4. Drain off your chicken broth (DON'T RINSE).
5. Add butter and bacon. Heat up for a couple minutes and serve.

SMOTHERED MEAT

by Pam

This is a most requested recipe at our family reunions, especially made with round steak. Very easy and delicious

Prep Time: **30 min.** | Cook Time: **1.5 hrs.** | Oven Temp: **350° F**

INGREDIENTS

4-6 Pieces Pork Chops, Chicken or Round Steak
2 c. Flour
⅓ c. Oil
Season Salt to taste
Black Pepper to taste
Garlic Powder to taste
Paprika to taste
2 cans Cream of Mushroom soup
½ c. Milk, more if needed

INSTRUCTIONS:

1. Mix your seasonings, season salt, black pepper, garlic powder and paprika with 2 cups of flower.
2. Dredge your meat in flour mixture.
3. Mix 2 cans of cream of mushroom soup.
4. Fry your dredged meat in approximately ½ cup of oil until brown. Preferably a cast iron skillet. If you don't have one, any skillet will do.
5. Place browned meat in a 9 x 13 casserole dish, side by side.
6. Pour Soup mixture over the meat.
7. Cover with foil or a lid. Bake approx. 1 1/2 hours on 350°F.

DISPATCH SHENANIGANS

by Pam

We do have slow shifts. We must entertain ourselves to keep our minds sharp. Below are some things we did to keep us sharp! Well, that is what we called it.

We had a dispatcher that would do anything for a laugh. We pin curled her hair, put a windsock on her head, and ran up and down the hallways. Very good laugh that day! But we pulled pranks on her too. She was known to chug her Pepsi. You would think she wouldn't do that when she would find hot sauce, salt, and who knows what else was put in her Pepsi. Yes, that Pepsi would blow out of her nose and spew out of her mouth. She is missed. RIP Connie.

We had some hot games of Euchre. Exciting games of Uno. And other board games we accumulated over the years. We put together puzzles too.

We have made up Easter Baskets for other Dispatchers Children, from the Easter Bunny

We have had a mad wrapping table set up in the middle of the center for Santa Claus Presents. If you were not on a call, you were wrapping presents on Christmas Eve.

We had metal gun boxes the deputies had to put their weapons in before entering the secure part of our facility. We also used them to pass items back and forth between the Jail office and our dispatch center. There have been some very interesting items put in that box……..lit firecrackers for one, that'll wake you up really quick.

On the third shift, you only had one food establishment open. And it was about 10 miles away. We would ask the deputies to relay our food to us. Sometimes we got it; sometimes we didn't. If we didn't get it, the deputy had chucked it out the window going to a hot call. If we did get it, a lot of times, if you had a sandwich, there was a big ol' bite out of it. HA

Many times, the Deputies would ask to run a car plate. Sure enough, it would be YOUR PLATE. The deputy would advise us that this car/plate was North Bound on a US 31.

We always had pitch-ins for holidays or just because. You can bet we celebrated Birthdays with a big spread. Of course, there were times, we were trying to plan the SURPRISE PARTY, and the Birthday girl/guy would walk in, and we all looked like the cat who ate the canary. And just start talking gibberish.

Our phones also had an intercom system to the entire facility. Yes, one of the old farm books that make sounds was played over that intercom system several times in a row. And, yes, the Sheriff himself walked to our Dispatch center and advised us he was in a meeting and to please stop playing that nonsense over the intercom. That's the polite version of that conversation, HA

And of course, your Radio Mics would get stuck open. People have heard dispatch sing Christmas carols, talk about going home to a bubble bath, painting their nails. And some curse words actually went out several times.

Now through all of this, we never missed a call of help. You see, we indeed do have the heart and mindset of community service and a deep devotion to helping those in need.

SHORTS

by Pam

Every new dispatcher got tested, and/or initiated, in one way or another…..

Deputy P, would call in and whisper, "help me, " " help me". He had a creepy way of doing this, and it was so good it even creeps me out. Of course, they tried to get an address and do as much as they could for the caller, and that's all he would say. After a few moments, he would hang up. The new dispatcher would then start the process for trying to call the caller back. But before they could attempt this. Deputy P, would call back in and talk to that Dispatcher, they would have a great laugh, and he gave them all passing grades.

I was training a new hire one early morning. I assigned her to a radio channel and sat with her to monitor her progress. We had dispatched an officer to a welfare check, and he said over the air to her, "Dispatch, we have two dead bodies". She proceeded to push off the console in her rolling chair, saying I can't take this call. I immediately rolled her back in front of the radio and told her, "yes, you can." She immediately rolled backward again, I immediately pushed her back in front of that radio. Eventually, she knew this job wasn't for her. Well, you never know.

The officers would run the new dispatcher's car tags over the air and advise the new dispatcher that this vehicle was speeding on a certain road. When they ran their car plates and realized it was their car, they were like, now what do I do? I would tell them, read all that information as loud and proud as you can, even if it is your car and they pranked ya!

And, when I was new, my trainer, Lynne, made me start talking on the radio with a broadcast. It was a speeding Semi, northbound on one of our Interstates. So, I proceeded with the description with a quiver in my voice. A White 58 INCH semi, with a yellow cab, speeding northbound " Yes, I said inch. Of course, the radio lit up with responses. "Dispatch, was that a semi by Tonka"? Of course it was 58 feet. But I sucked it up and corrected myself on the air. HAHA, I never lived that one down for a while.

But something was always going on in that room. Whether it was the Officers who got a case of the stutters, not once, not twice but 3 or 4 transmissions, then they couldn't talk because they were laughing at themselves, and then it was catchy, the Dispatcher would have the giggles.

When our radio microphones would stick open, there were many songs sung over the radio. My songs were "Baby Let's Twist again like we did Last Summer," "Feliz Navidad" and "I got friends in low places" Of course, no one would call to let you know your Microphone was open until after you had sung almost the entire song !!!

And, yes, we can't forget when you were gossiping or talking about another dispatcher, the mic would ALWAYS be open. HA.

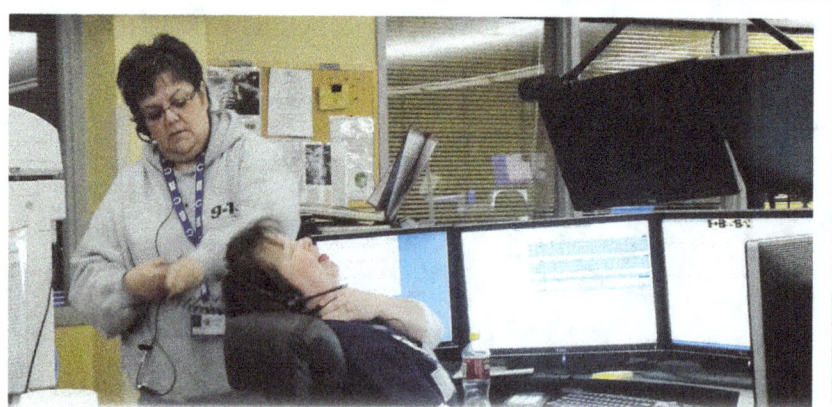

Pam had had enough of Missy's constant chatter and singing for the day. Everyone in the room clapped as she choked Missy with her console plug in cord.

AFTER SCHOOL COOKIES

by Pam

My Mother, Mabel, would make these for us after school, or when we had a big kick ball tournament in front of house. She doubled the recipe for both teams! Always served with Kool-Aid !!

Prep Time: **12 min.**

INGREDIENTS

- 2 c. Peanut Butter
- ½ c. Powder Sugar
- 1 Tbsp. Butter
- 4 Tbsps. Honey
- 1 tsp. Vanilla
- Graham Crackers (Use Cinnamon Graham Crackers, or regular Graham Crackers)

INSTRUCTIONS:

1. Add Butter and Honey along with Peanut Butter and Vanilla.
2. Add powdered sugar slowly, mixing thoroughly. You want the consistency of a sandwich cookie filling. It will set up as it sits If to thin, add some more powdered sugar. If too thick, add a very small amount of water.
3. Scoop onto Cinnamon, or regular Graham Crackers.
4. Top with another graham cracker, press down to spread out the peanut butter mixture.
5. Sometimes my Mom would add grape jelly to make a PBJ cookie!

DAYNA'S WACKY CAKE

by Pam

Of course, working in Dispatch, you worked Major Holidays, Birthdays, weekends etc etc. Many times we would have a pitch in breakfast/lunch/dinner depending on your shift. This cake was always brought by Dayna. We loved it. Dayna worked in Dispatch and as a Reserve officer for many, many years. RIP Dayna we miss & love you MEH !

Prep Time: **15 min.** | *Cook Time:* **30 hrs.** | *Oven Temp:* **350° F**

INGREDIENTS

- 1 ½ c. Flour
- ¾ c. Sugar
- 1/3 c. Unsweetened Cocoa
- 1 tsp. Baking Soda
- ½ tsp. Salt
- 1/3 c. Oil
- 1 Tbsp. White Vinegar
- 2 tsp. Vanilla extract
- 1 c. Water

INSTRUCTIONS:

1. Sift flour, sugar, cocoa, baking soda and salt into an ungreased 8x8 pan; spread your sifted dry ingredients evenly in the pan.
2. Then, make a large well (hole), and 2 small wells in your dry mixture. Carefully pour the oil into the large well, vinegar into 1 of the small wells, and vanilla into the remaining well
3. Pour 1 cup of water evenly over the entire mixture in your pan.
4. Stir everything together with a fork until combined.
5. Preheat oven to 350 degrees.
6. Bake approx 30 mins. Cool.
7. After cooled, you can cover in powdered sugar, or icing of your choice. Or no icing at all. It's very moist.

GIRL

by Pam

I once took a call in dispatch from a little girl who was about 4 or 5 years old. She said that she could not find her mom and dad. I asked her where she saw them last, and she said they went to the bedroom. But she said that her mom told her that if the door was shut she should not open it unless it was an emergency. I asked her if she had an emergency: was she sick? injured? etc.

"No," she said. "I just want something to drink."

"Well, let's go knock on the bedroom door," I told her. "Don't open it. Just knock on it and take this phone with you."

So she did. She knocked on the door, and I heard her mom ask if something was wrong. I told the little girl to tell mommy that the police wanted to talk to her, and she obeyed again. Mom was immediately on the phone. I told her the story and asked her if everything was ok, because I had police started that way to make sure everything was alright.

Mom started giggling and giggling and told me that yes, everything was ok - and to please call off the police that were en route.

But of course I couldn't stop the police. So they completed the call, and the officer advised that everything was alright - just "husband/wife stuff," was the report.

CORNBREAD DRESSING

by Pam

This was a staple for us at Thanksgiving and Christmas. We normally made our own cornbread, but came to love the boxed cornbread, made it quicker and easier.

Prep Time: **30 min.** | Cook Time: **1 hr.** | Oven Temp: **400° F**

INGREDIENTS

1 sm Box Cornbread Mix

3 Stalks Celery

1 sm Onion

1 Tbsp. Butter

4+ c. Chicken or Turkey Broth

2 Eggs, Beaten

1 tsp. Sage (optional)

½ loaf White Bread

Black Pepper to taste

INSTRUCTIONS:

1. Mix and bake cornbread as directed on the box.
2. Chop celery & onion saute' in butter till soft.
3. Crumble white bread & cornbread into a large mixing bowl.
4. Add onion, celery to your cornbread/white bread mix. Start adding your 4 cups of broth. (if you are baking a turkey, use that broth, much richer flavor, add chicken broth to it, to make 4 cups.).
5. Add 2 beaten eggs to the broth/bread mix. add sage and black pepper. Mix very well, you want this mixture to be very moist.
6. Pour into a large baking pan, or 2, 9x13 baking pans
7. Bake at 400 degrees 45 minutes to an hour.

PIG

by Pam

I worked the midnight shift for about six years as a dispatcher. If something big was going to happen, it always seemed to happen during third shift, and I loved being part of the action.

One winter night, about 3:00 a.m., I was on duty and received a call about a traffic hazard in the street.

"What is the nature of the hazard?" I asked the caller.

"There is a large pig walking down the road, and it is wearing a red & white Indiana University sweater," came the reply.

Flabbergasted and amused, I dispatched the run to a good friend of mine, and there was dead silence on the other end when I relayed the call.

"Dispatch, could you please repeat," he finally said.

So, I did.

"That's what I thought you said, dispatch," he replied. "Glad he has his sweater on. It's cold out here! I'll be en route to check the area." I chuckled, as he knew I would.

The officer did find him: 200 pounds of potbellied pig just walking right down the center of the road.

We finally found his owners, and the pig was returned home - safe, sound, and warm.

HAM 'N BEANS

by Pam

This is my go to recipe when this weather turns cold. Warms you up quick !

Prep Time: **5 min.** | Cook Time: **10 hrs.** | Oven Temp: **375° F**

INGREDIENTS

2 c. Dry White Beans or Pinto Beans

1 med. Onion, Diced

1 Ham Hock

4 c. Water or Chicken Broth or a mixture of both

Black Pepper to taste

INSTRUCTIONS:

1. You really need to soak your dry beans overnight in baking soda. Makes them very tender, and less gassy!!
2. After beans have soaked overnight, rinse them off in the morning Combine, beans, chopped up onion, ham hock, and chicken stock/water.
3. Put your entire bean mixture in your crock pot. Add more or less chicken stock, depends if you want a lot of juice or not, I normally cover mine with chicken stock. C
4. over with black pepper. Cook 8-10 hrs on low, 6-8 hours on high in the crockpot
5. Drop in a few egg noodles if you want at the end, cook another 20 mins if you do this.

Delicious served with cornbread.

HOW DEAD IS HE?

by Pam

I had only been on duty at the dispatch center for less than an hour, early one morning, when the 911 phone lit up. I was only one coffee into the day and still hadn't quite woken up all the way. But I quicklyI answered.

"911, what's your emergency?"

I heard an elderly man's voice, but before I could say anything and without a pause, he proceeded to tell me that he hadn't seen his neighbor in several days. He was very calm and articulate, with no trace of urgency in his voice. Typically when we receive a call from such a calm person, there is nothing to be concerned about. Neighbors often look out for one another, of course. So I continued the conversation without much concern about a true emergency situation.

"Do you suspect anything is wrong?" I asked him.

In a non-urgent tone, once again, the caller said, "Well ma'am, I walked over to his house this morning to check on him. The door was unlocked, so I opened the door and found him dead on the floor."

I was taken aback, after the man's calm demeanor thus far, and I switched into full emergency mode: confirming the address, getting names, and starting the ambulance and medics. Finally I came to the point in our protocol where I needed to assess the danger and whether the caller could start CPR or some other medical attention.

Now, in my head, I wanted to say, "How does it appear that he has died?" But what came out of my mouth was, "How dead is he?"

Again the gentleman caller responded in a very calm voice, "Well ma'am, he's pretty dead. He's blue."

After I completed this call and the situation had been handled, I had to laugh at myself a little - not for the situation of course, but for what I said to that poor man who took me so seriously and responded so serenely.

And then I had to go drink more coffee!

CREAM PIE

by Pam

This is out of an old Church recipe book. I've been making this for Christmas at least 25 years. So, so good. Sometimes I will add a little extra Vanilla Enjoy !

Prep Time: **15 min.** | Cook Time: **15 min.** | Oven Temp: **375° F**

INGREDIENTS

¼ c. Cornstarch

1 c. Sugar

1 c. Milk

1 c. Half & Half

1 Stick butter, cut into lumps

1 tsp. Vanilla

Cinnamon/Nutmeg

1 Pre-Cooked Pie Shell

INSTRUCTIONS:

1. In a sauce pan, mix cornstarch and sugar; add milk & half & half.
2. Stir over medium heat till thick; remove from heat.
3. Add butter and Vanilla.
4. Pour mixture into your precooked pie shell Sprinkle with Cinnamon &/or Nutmeg to your taste.
5. Bake 20 minutes at 375 degrees

GOULASH

by Pam

I once dispatched 158 accidents in an 8-hour shift, on a first snowfall day. I remember vividly making this when I got home. I needed something quick, easy and most of all comforting. I was wore out, physically and mentally.

Prep Time: **10 min.** | *Cook Time:* **45 hrs.**

INGREDIENTS

- 1 lb. Hamburger
- 3 c. Tomato Juice or Beef Broth
- 15 oz. can Stewed Tomatoes
- 2 c. Macaroni
- ½ brick Velveeta
- Garlic Powder to taste
- Salt to taste
- Black Pepper to taste

INSTRUCTIONS:

1. Fry your hamburger with salt, garlic powder and black pepper.
2. Drain well on a paper towel.
3. Put your hamburger in your dutch oven, fill with 3 cups of tomato juice (my preference) or 3 Cups of Beef broth, or a mix of both. add 15 oz can of stewed tomatoes
4. Add 2 cups of already cooked macaroni (we liked a lot of macaroni, you may want to adjust the amount your cook)
5. Cook covered about 30 mins.
6. Then add 1/2 brick of Velveeta in chunks so it melts easier.

I like to add BBQ sauce to mine once in the bowl.

PASTA SALAD

by Pam

This is an excellent pitch-in salad. Play around with the veggies you want to add. Black olives, salami, pepperoni would be good added. You can even add some shredded Parmesan Cheese. This recipe is easily doubled, or halved down in size, depending on the amount of people you will be serving

Prep Time: **20 min.** | *Cook Time:* **20 min.**

INGREDIENTS

- 12 oz box Tri Color Rotini
- ½ Green Bell Pepper, Chopped
- ½ Red Bell Pepper, Chopped
- ½ Yellow Bell Pepper, Chopped
- ½ C Grape Tomatoes, halved
- ½ Red Onion, Chopped
- 1 lg. Cucumber
- 1 sm. bottle Wishbone Zesty Robusto
- Salt, Pepper and Garlic Powder to taste

INSTRUCTIONS:

1. Cook Rotini pasta per package directions. Drain and rinse with cold water to stop the cooking process. You don't want your pasta mushy.
2. In a large mixing bowl, combine all ingredients gently toss all ingredients till thoroughly mixed.
3. Cover and chill at the minimum for 2 hours.

911 Emergency Dispatchers, Public Safety Responders

SWEET POTATOES

by Pam

Prep Time: **5 min.**

INGREDIENTS

5 Sweet Potatoes, regular size
½ c. Evaporated Milk
1 c. Brown Sugar
¼ c. Melted Butter
2 Eggs, Beaten
1 tsp. Cinnamon
½ tsp. Nutmeg
Pinch Salt
Marshmallows, To taste

INSTRUCTIONS:

1. Peel sweet Potato's. Boil till tender, 20 mins ?
2. Mash your sweet potatoes with a blender, till smooth
3. Add evaporated milk, brown sugar, melted butter, 2 beaten eggs, cinnamon, nutmeg, vanilla and salt
4. Bake your sweet potato mixture in a 9x 13 pan, (or smaller, depending on how thick your want your casserole) for around 20 minutes
5. Remove casserole from oven . Cover the entire top with Marshmallows
6. Put back in the oven, till the marshmallows are browned. Serve.

FRIED CORN

by Pam

We really looked forward to this during the summer when corn came in. Delicious with sliced tomatoes and fresh green beans.

Prep Time: **10 min.** | Cook Time: **45 hrs.**

INGREDIENTS

8 ears Corn
4 Tbsp. Butter, more if desired
Salt and Pepper to taste
Splash Milk, Cream, Half & Half
1 tsp. Sugar
2 Strips of Bacon + grease

INSTRUCTIONS:

1. Cut your corn off the cob. Milk the corn cob with the back, flat edge of your knife.
2. Fry your bacon and remove from pan. Leave your bacon grease in the pan and add ½ the butter.
3. Add the corn, cook around 10 minutes, and add the rest of the butter. Depending on the thickness you want, add some milk.
4. Add your salt & pepper

RIDE A LONGS

by Pam

When I started dispatching, we were required to go on "ride-alongs" with our officers to learn the areas of the county we would be dispatching for. One of the first officers I rode with was our K-9 officer on a midnight shift. He asked if there was a certain place I wanted to visit, and I told him there was something I had heard a lot about: Screaming Bridge. There was a lot of folklore about murders there, so I was intrigued and he was obliging.

When we got to the bridge, the officer stopped in the middle of it and acted like his car broke down. It was the middle of the night, and here we were in nowhere land. I suspected he was fooling with me about the car, but then all of the sudden there was a large THUMP. Needless to say, I screamed like a little girl, and he just laughed at me because Sonny--his eighty pound German Shepard--had decided just at the right time to plop down and take a nap!

I became good friends with this officer and rode with him quite often during our midnight shift. He would meet up with other K-9 officers, and they would put me in the training sleeve and have me hide behind dumpsters, trees, and bushes so that their dogs could train to find me. And even though it was a lot of fun, I still couldn't help but wonder about the large percentage of my body that wasn't covered by that sleeve!

One night we were dispatched to a fatality accident on a rural county road: two teenage girls had been killed. No one was on the scene yet except for me and the officer I was riding with when suddenly the parents of the girls showed up. This was absolutely horrible. I had to assist the officer in keeping them from the scene until the fire department came, and this was one of my first heart wrenching experiences as a dispatcher--which, even though I didn't really know it then, would come quite often over the years.

One of the most exciting ride-alongs was with an officer I liked to call "Uncle Billy Willy," though he'd answer to just about anything. We were in a pursuit for maybe four or five miles on a two-lane interstate. It was a drunk driver who was obviously inebriated. He would cross the median, go Northbound in the Southbound lane, cross the median again, and then go the opposite direction. Of course, I had NEVER been in a vehicle going this fast, and when we had to cross the median the first time, Uncle Billy Willy giggled and yelled: "Hold on to your ass Fred," in good ol' Smokey & the Bandit style. Now that was exciting! No one was injured, no vehicles were damaged, and the drunk driver was arrested.

Becky made Pam's birthday cake.

POLICE OFFICER BIO

Robert Jeffries. I prefer to go by Bob. I was born on November 26, 1950, at a naval base hospital where my father was stationed at the Quonset Point Naval Base in Rhode Island. My parents divorced when I was 5 years old, and my grandmother arrived by train and took me back to Carmel, Indiana, where I grew up. I graduated from Carmel High School in 1968.

While working as the marshal in the town of Atlanta, I met my wife Lisa when she was working at the local O'Malia's Food Market. It was the only place in town to get a sandwich made at the deli meat counter, and, needless to say, I ate a lot of deli meat sandwiches so I could see her. We dated for a few months before I asked to marry me, and we were married on July 1, 1977. Lisa started her career as a dispatcher after we were married. Since I was the town marshal, the police department phone rang into our house because I would be on duty 24 hours a day, seven days a week. This gave her the experience to start her career with the Hamilton County Sheriff's Department, under then Sheriff Bob Chandler. Being on call seven days a week, 24 hours a day was challenging, and I felt that moving to a larger department would be an advantage for Lisa and me.

I had the opportunity to be hired at the Noblesville Police Department and started there in October, 1977, as a patrolman on second shift from 2:00 p.m. to 10:00 a.m. for my first 18 months. Then I was promoted to Sergeant in late 1978 and worked the late shift from 10:00 p.m. to 6:00 a.m. for the next five years. From 1983-1985, I was assigned to work as the only investigator on staff. Then my role advanced to Lieutenant, and I was in charge of the late shift. On January 1, 1989, I was promoted to Major/Assistant Chief and worked in that role until

October, 1995, at which time I reverted back to my former rank of Lieutenant.

A highlight of my career was attending the FBI National Academy in Quantico, Virginia, where I studied investigative courses, criminal law, and criminal gangs, along with specialized photography. During my time at the FBI Academy, I had the opportunity to take a trip to the BIG city of New York, and our group was escorted on a VIP tour of the city. One of the standout moments was our visit to the Twin Towers, which had just reopened from a terrorist attack that bombed the parking garages. We rode elevators to the observation deck and could view the city in all directions, taking many great pictures for good memories of that visit. I graduated from the academy in December, 1995, and returned to work as the second shift lieutenant for a year until switching to third shift, which I held for the next eight years.

In January, 2004, I was assigned to start our agency on a national accreditation program for CALEA (Commission on Accreditation for Law Enforcement Agencies). This took up my time until I retired on March 1, 2006. Lisa and I had three children in our marriage of 44 years (as of July 1, 2021). Our first son, Cortney, was born February 21, 1980, and our second son, Christopher, was born July 24, 1984. Our daughter was born June 18, 1991. As a family we loved to take vacations to Florida, where the kids enjoyed Disney World and Busch Gardens in Tampa. We also took up camping as a hobby and traveled to many different campgrounds, though our favorites were always in Kentucky. We explored many small towns on our camping trips and enjoyed visiting antique shops we found there. We have always looked forward to being grandparents, and on April 20, 2021, we were blessed with our first granddaughter. Lisa and I look forward to having many wonderful years with her and hope the day will come when we have other grandchildren to enjoy life with as well.

FLIPPED ME THE BIRD

by Bob

In the early days of third shift in the late '70s, many times it was only me and one other officer--a two-car shift to protect the entire city. Many nights it was quiet and this allowed us more time to watch for burglary suspects and various other crimes. On other nights, however, we discovered that there were always plenty of foolish people who wanted our attention, and we were always happy to give it to them.

In the area of SR 38 & SR 32, Nick (the other officer) radioed me and said he had a car drive by and flip him the middle finger. We decided to follow this driver and then pulled the car over just N of SR 32 on a side street. As luck would have it, we could smell the distinct odor of marijuana coming from inside the car. We cuffed them and were then sure to mention that their trip to jail was courtesy of their wanting and getting our attention.

IMPAIRED DRIVERS

by Bob

I spent 18 years of my 28 years as a police officer working the late shift. Not surprisingly, much of my time during that shift was spent watching for impaired drivers. The prime times were 2:30-3:15 a.m. to catch those leaving early and those waiting for their last call servings.

Once I was working the west side of the city when I saw two cars with one following the other closely. I knew that impaired drivers do this on occasion to help the one who is the most drunk get home. So, I started to follow the two cars as they turned south on Cherry Tree Road. This particular road has some really interesting and challenging "S" curves. I turned on my in-car video and started my observations of these two. They soon proved my instincts right as they were weaving between the lanes - an obvious sign of being intoxicated.

After another mile or so, one car split off into a driveway while the other took off at a fast pace, obviously thinking it was the cops on their tail. It was time to stop this person, because I knew that I had enough video to back up probable cause. So I turned on the red and blues and followed the car, which was already driving at high speeds as I chased him down a narrow country road. We were going in excess of 70 MPH, with the "S" curves coming up quickly ahead of us.

The driver slowed down a little to make the first curve and somehow skidded through it, with me in pursuit. But the second curve is more difficult. He went too wide and hit the guide wire from a power pole, launching his car vertically off the pavement and into the air. I jumped out and jerked the driver's door open to get him out of his vehicle. Sure enough, he was intoxicated. So I put on the cuffs and placed him in my car to take him to the county jail.

On the way we had a bit of small talk, and he paid me a compliment: "Man, you really can drive!"

To which I replied: "It makes a big difference when you aren't drunk!"

BALL PYTHON

by Bob

Often, when a night on police duty has been too quiet, something strange is bound to happen. One warm summer night when I was working third shift, a radio dispatch was sent out telling the area police car of a call on East Maple Street. The call was from a man who said he was feeding his ball python snake, and it had swallowed his hand and wrapped itself around his body. His friends who were there refused to help him. After the information came out, the radio was silent.

I figured someone had to go, and I wasn't really afraid of snakes, plus by this time I was a little curious about the situation. So I responded, "En route." On arrival, I entered the apartment, and sure enough, there was a man wrapped up by a Ball Python, with his hand inside its mouth. The snake looked about 12-14 feet long and as big around as my leg. The man explained that he had fed the snake a rabbit and after it had finished eating, he reached in the aquarium and it struck out at him, swallowing his whole hand!

Obviously drunk and very concerned about his snake not being harmed, the man made me promise to just help put the snake back in its aquarium. So I grabbed the tail and began to unwind the snake from his body. Finally, the last step was to get his hand out. So he pulled, and it popped out. Then we both carried the snake over and put it back in the aquarium.

My fellow officers later thanked me for taking a job they definitely did not want to do!

APPLIANCE STORE

by Bob

It was a lazy night during a winter shift and not much had taken place. Even criminals sometimes stay inside! About 3:00 a.m. we were dispatched to investigate an alarm at a local tire and appliance store. Joe, Nick, and I were the officers on duty that night, and all of us responded to the alarm. Nick found that the store had been broken into, with fresh footprints in the snow leading west from the building. As the lead that night, Nick followed the tracks for two blocks west to where they ended at a mobile home. Inside he could see movement from two men putting things inside the refrigerator and stove. He radioed Joe and me and related to us what he observed. Then all three of us waited.

After it looked like they had hidden the stolen items and settled down, we knocked on the door. When they answered, we asked if we could come in and talk to them. Then we explained that we were investigating a burglary and asked permission to search their home.

Surprisingly, permission was granted, and we quickly found microwaves and other appliances hidden inside the refrigerator and inside the oven. Other items were recovered from the bedrooms. Some offenders sure make our job easy!

SEE MY BROTHER

by Bob

It was early one third shift, shortly after I had been appointed sergeant, when dispatch contacted me and said that a man called to state he was coming to the police department with a knife to his throat and would kill himself if he wasn't allowed to see his brother in jail. We were just starting to talk about how wild this seemed when, to our amazement, in walked the man, holding a pocket knife to his throat and demanding to see his brother.

As the sergeant, I was in charge, so I had to come up with a plan - quickly! I decided that trying to negotiate with him would be the best way to hopefully achieve compliance and safety. So I put him in my police car and started driving to the jail. Dispatch called ahead of us to the jail and found that, as luck would have it, off-duty Officer Brown was at the jail, and he agreed to sit in the lobby until I arrived.

Driving up Conner Street, almost to the jail, I nearly chose to slam on the brakes and try to disarm my desperate passenger. But that was risky, so I decided against that plan and proceeded to the jail parking lot. We entered the jail lobby, and the man demanded once again to see his brother. As we stood at the door, waiting for it to open, Officer Brown seized the opportunity and dove onto the man. Then I helped Brown tackle him to the floor. We were able to get the knife away from him, and thankfully the tense situation ended with no injuries.

"Now you can go inside to be with your brother," we told him.

WE BOTH SCREAM

by Bob

It was another summer night of third shift in the city, and things were not especially hopping that evening. I was in the downtown area, and a fellow officer, Joe, was in the north part of the city. He radioed that he would be out at the soccer fields near the railroad tracks with a vehicle and two occupants. I started heading his way as back up when he radioed that he had one apprehension and one subject on foot running south on the railroad tracks towards town.

Ok, I figured, this subject would likely try to make it back to town and call someone to come get him. Joe couldn't chase him because he had a prisoner, so I tried to use my head and find a place to hide and wait for this man to come to me. So, I drove to Forest Hill School on Lake View Drive and parked my car so it couldn't be seen. I walked to the railroad tracks that run between the school and Forest Park, and I hid beside a tree.

It was really dark, not much light to see, but in about 10 minutes I could hear the crunching of gravel on the railroad tracks from a person running. When it sounded like he had gotten to my location, I jumped out and screamed, "Halt! Police!" Taken by surprise, he screamed, too - and then slumped down, worn out from running all that distance. There was no resistance from him as I handcuffed him and walked him to my car. Then I radioed Joe that I had his man!

BREAKING INTO CARS

by Bob

It seems like warm summer nights on third shift patrol always yielded some of the most interesting finds when I was a police officer. Around 3:00 a.m. one night, another officer and I were sitting in our cars in a parking lot in the 600 block of Conner Street. We happened to notice a man whom we both were familiar with as a local multi-time thief walking out from the dark by the Conner Street bridge. He was carrying what looked like a tool box, and as he crossed the street he continued south.

We both fired up our patrol cars and headed over to our suspect. Then we lit up our lights and stopped him. We found that he had items on him from breaking into cars in the north end of town. We eventually discovered that these items belong to a local attorney. I was well aware of how attorneys love to get clients from among criminal offenders and make money from defending these poor misguided people. So, as fate would have it, I had city court the next week, and the attorney whose stolen property we recovered happened to be in court.

"Hey," I said to him, "I've got a prospective client for you!"

"You do?" he replied.

So I told him

SYPHON GAS

by Bob

In late summer, when gas prices are often high, criminals would never buy their gas but would syphon it from other cars. This became a big problem at times. In one instance, I was on duty with another officer - just the two of us working the whole city. We were spent quite a bit of time that night driving around the city trying to track down gas thefts. Usually we would show up just in time to find the can left behind and the rubber hose running to it, but no suspect in sight.

Ok, we have to do things differently, we thought. Then a call came that a gas theft was in progress on the southwest side of town. So it was time to implement our new strategies.

We drove to within a block of the call then turned off our lights and parked our cars. We proceeded on foot, creeping through the yards of homes near the call. Eventually we could see

a young man about 6 feet tall standing by the car with his gas can on the ground and rubber hose running from the car's gas tank to his can. This was our moment.

We very quietly snuck up behind the perpetrator and yelled, "Surprise!"

As he turned to see two cops in uniform, he screamed in shock, and we grabbed him and placed handcuffs on him. To our delight, it looked like we had come up with a new way to fight this type of crime!

FIREFIGHTER BIO

Stephen Harold Haston. I was born in Indianapolis, Indiana, on September 19, 1960, to Irivia June Haston and Harold Maurice Haston, a World War II veteran. Steve has four younger brothers. "Five boys," my Mom and Dad would say, "we have our own basketball team!" I was not very good at basketball, but I did excel at the martial arts. When I was young, my dad would teach me all of the karate and fighting techniques he learned in the war. Of course, this was the era of the martial arts movies, and my brothers and I practiced every move we watched. After graduating from Northwest High School in Indianapolis, I went to work at a 400,000 square foot warehouse as a forklift operator, moving pallets of books that were bound for schools across the globe. With my first check, I joined Olympic Karate Studio. During the next several years, I worked and practiced karate. By the early 1980s I had competed in dozens of tournaments all over the state, winning enough matches to have reached "number one" in sparring.

One evening while at the karate dojo, a 19-year-old woman named Missy walked past me and my brother as we were sitting on the floor stretching. My little brother, who was 12 years old, said, "Oh, I am going to date her." My reply was "Dude, I'm going around you; she is mine!" Well, Missy is one of our authors for this book, and yes, she and I have been married for 36 years. After we married, I had to get a real job, so I applied to the Noblesville Fire Department (NFD) and was hired on January 16, 1987 - just 12 days after Missy gave birth to our first child. I remember the hard first day: Missy was crying, I was crying, the baby was crying, everybody was crying. I almost didn't go.

But I did, and for the next eight years, I was a back stepper, meaning I was fighting fires. This was the early '80s, so we still rode on the back bumper of the fire engine for runs. My very first fire run was to a detached garage. I put my gear on, jumped on the back bumper, and we were off, lights and sirens! I was so excited. No one told me how bumpy the ride was going to be on the back. Holy smokes! The first bump in the road almost knocked me off. The fireman beside me was laughing so hard that I could barely hear him tell me to hold on tight and bend my knees. That was fun, scary, dangerous, and crazy, all at the same time (though before the end of my first year, the back bumper riding was banned).

After eight years as a firefighter, I applied for the position of Hazardous Materials Coordinator and was appointed to the position. I switched to a 40-hour work week, which was a big adjustment after eight years of 24-hour shift work. For the next two years, I worked very hard at growing the hazmat program. I took many classes in chemistry, air monitoring, sampling, incident command, radiation, decon, and more. I wanted to incorporate as many of these areas as possible in the program, not only to make the Noblesville Fire Department a premier hazmat response team but also to enhance the safety of responders and citizens.

About two years into the hazmat gig, the city mayor changed, which often means that most of the upper governmental positions change, too. The fire chief and deputy chiefs were removed. I was blessed that my hazmat position was not touched; in fact, I was asked if I had an interest in becoming the Chief of Operations to combine hazmat with operations. I did think and pray about it, and after a few days, I took the position. For the next seven years, I worked with a great team of firefighters and served well in my job. Together we added new programs, expanded our capabilities, added BLS ambulance service, improved safety, created community outreach programs, and more.

Eventually, like my predecessors, I could sense that my time as the Operations Chief was coming to an end. I knew the upcoming election would change the course of things. One Friday night at 4:15, just before our 4:30 quitting time, the fire chief walked into my office. He made a little small talk and then said, "Well, bud, the mayor and I think we will not need you as the Operations Chief any longer. I am going to re-assign you back to a crew, but you can have a few days off to figure everything out." I told him thanks for the 15-minute notice! While not very funny at the time, this change later turned out to be a blessing.

I was assigned to station 74 as the ladder engineer and fire/rescue boat operator. I had extensive training in both of the positions. Also, the new fire chief allowed me to remain as the hazardous materials coordinator. For the next 12 years or so, I stayed in these positions, making many fire and rescue runs and managing the hazmat team. Through all of the ups and downs, the Noblesville Fire Department was good to me, and I think I was good to them. After 28 years of serving the community, the time came for me to retire. In September of 2015, I did just that. My plan was to spend time with my family, work around the house, and babysit my two grandchildren. This lasted for one year. A position with Hamilton County Emergency Management (HCEM) had opened up, and I was interested. I had been a member of this organization for the entire time I was with the fire department as a volunteer. I was delighted when they hired me as a full-time coordinator, almost one year to the day after retiring from the NFD.

During my years with HCEM I have been the Volunteer Program Coordinator, LEPC Lead Planner, Asset and Equipment Manager, and currently the Unmanned Aerial Aircraft Program Manager. I now have a combined 34 years of public service to the community, and I have many stories to tell. I am delighted to be a contributor to this book - part storybook and part cookbook. When my wife came up with this idea, I immediately thought it was a great one. After all, my work experiences did always make me think of something to eat after the run was over! The stories I tell in this book are true, and I am confident that when you read them and look at the recipe that goes with each one, you will enjoy the connections, too.

FAMILY ROAST

by Steve

At the fire house we always took turns cooking. That allowed many opportunities for experimenting with food. Sometimes the experiments went bad, lol. So feel free to alter the ingredient quantities to meet our taste. This roast is one of my creations and I think it is pretty good. I have used grape seed oil or avocado oil even coconut oil, you decide. It is easy to throw it all in the oven or even a crock pot. It is a hearty meal and will fill you and the family up.

Prep Time: **20 min.** | *Cook Time:* **3 hrs.** | *Oven Temp:* **325° F**

INGREDIENTS

- 3-4 lbs. Beef Roast
- 2 c. Beef Stock
- ¼ c. All Purpose Flour
- 4 Tbsp. Grape Seed Oil
- 4 cloves Garlic, minced
- 4 sprigs Thyme
- 2 Bay Leaves
- 1 Onion
- 1 Red Pepper
- Salt and Pepper to taste
- 3 lbs. Small Red Potatoes
- 2 lbs. Baby Carrots

INSTRUCTIONS

1. In a bowl, combine your choice of flour, salt and pepper.
2. Preheat oven to 325 degrees. Note: You can use a crock pot if you prefer.
3. Begin heating a large pan on medium high heat.
4. Oil evenly the roast and then coat the entire roast in the mixture.
5. Add the roast to the heated pan and cook for 5 minutes on each side. Remove roast from pan.
6. Reduce the pan heat to low. Add garlic, thyme, bay leaf, onion and red pepper. Cook for 4 minutes stirring frequently. Add beef stock to pan and bring to a boil.
7. Place the roast and contents from the pan in a oven roaster, also add the carrots and potatoes and cover. Place this in the oven for about 3 hours or until the roast is tender.
8. Remove thyme and bay leaf, discard and serve.

TWO MISSING THREE YEAR OLDS

by Steve

Anyone who has had a three-year-old child, or been around them, knows how angelic and cute they are - and also how amazingly fast, tricky, and cunning. In addition to my own children, I have experience with two different three year olds during my fire department service that proves this.

My encounter with the first child began on a summer afternoon at fire station 74. There were three of us on duty, and we had been working around the firehouse, cleaning and doing some maintenance. We all happened to be in the bay when the tones dropped for a run. Dispatch rattled off the incident: a missing three-year-old girl in a neighborhood about two miles northwest of the station. When there is an emergency involving a child, we are out the door even faster than usual, so we very quickly arrived at the girl's residence. I received instructions to set ladder 74 up next to the command post and extend the 75-foot ladder. It would serve as an elevated search platform. Multiple police officers, firefighters, and neighbors were already searching the area on foot. That area included many concerning terrain features like a lake, retention ponds, drain pipes, woods, and heavily-traveled roads.

My crew received our briefing: "Three-year-old girl last seen by mom in the home playing room. Mom told her to clean up her toys. She threw a fit, and mom told her to clean them up or she could not play with her friends outside. Mom went to the kitchen for just a minute, and when she came back, the little girl was gone."

Our assignment was to search the retention pond to the southwest. We immediately began our search of the shoreline and the underbrush, even crawling into the drain pipes. We were looking for all possible signs of where she may have entered the water, while praying that she did not. About 20 minutes into our search, we heard the Incident Commander come over the radio and say, "All units, you can return to service. The little girl has been found, safe and sound." We were all relieved!

After we returned to our stations, we called the commander to find out what exactly had happened. We learned that when the girl threw a fit, rather than going outside, she started pouting and basically went into stealth mode. She went upstairs to her parents' bedroom and somehow managed to crawl under the king mattress, cunningly not messing up the bed covers, and wedged herself between the two box springs. Then she just laid there quietly and fell asleep. The house had already been searched, but fortunately an officer decided to search it again. For some reason, even though the bed covers were perfectly made, the officer pulled the covers off the bed and looked under the mattress. Sure enough, there was the little sleeping angel!

My second three-year-old encounter was with a little boy. The dispatch read, "Ladder 74, assist police with a missing child at [address]." We immediately rushed to the ladder and made our way to the residence. No sooner had we arrived than the officers met us and reported that they had located the little boy. He had crawled to the back of a kitchen cabinet Lazy Susan and wedged himself in extraordinarily tight. He was flatly refusing to come out. Every time they tried to move the Lazy Susan, the boy screamed. So the mom, who was very frustrated with her son, had asked that we disassemble the Lazy Susan and deliver the little one to her. This boy was quite a piece of work! Whenever we tried to work on the on the Lazy Susan, he would shake the shelves, yell, and bang the pans around. It took us about 30 minutes, but we successfully extracted the boy and delivered him to his mommy's arms. He immediately transformed into a little angel. Oh you cute and crazy, three year olds!

APARTMENT ARSON FIRE

by Steve

It had been snowing for a few days, with a lot of snow and ice, and the temperature was around 21°. With the wind blowing, it felt like single digits outside. It was February, 1993, so the weather was par for the course in Indiana in the middle of winter. I remember going to the fire house that morning; the roads were a little rough, but there was less traffic for a Friday since we were under a travel advisory. I can remember thinking: I really hope we don't get any runs today, but with this kind of weather that's an unlikely wish to come true.

At the fire station, there were three of us coming on duty that day, so we sat down with the crew going off duty to shoot the breeze and get a morning briefing. To my delight, they told us that they didn't turn a wheel during the shift. If only we - and the citizens we serve - could get so lucky. We care a lot about the people we take care of. They are our neighbors, our friends, and we don't want them in danger. But if anything does happen, we will be there.

We spent the day making sure the fire engine was ready to go and shoveling the ramp so we could get out if needed. By 8:00 p.m., the three of us were winding down, and yes, it had been a quiet day. But that quiet was sadly going to be broken! Around 2:00 a.m. the tones dropped, awakening us. I knew it was bad the moment I heard the dispatcher's voice. We can usually tell because even though highly trained, dispatchers are human after all. This dispatcher's voice had all the makings of a serious incident; it was high and fast with a nervous rattle.

"Engine 71, Ladder 71, Rescue 71, Engine 72, report of an apartment fire [1234 Some St], Noble Manor Apartments, multiple people trapped."

As I was running for the engine and donning my bunker gear, I thought to myself, "This is bad, and the weather sucks, it is going to take station 71 and us a little longer to get there." As we were pulling out of the station and rolling, I heard dispatch give an update:

"Police are on the scene of a working apartment fire. Multiple people hanging out windows on all floors."

Now, we know just how bad it really is. I don't want to lose control of the engine on the icy road, but I told myself that I could do it, so I punched it. Not crazy, but a little more than the conditions warranted. It is always a balancing act; we can do no good at all if we don't make it there. It was less than a minute later when we heard Engine 71 mark "on scene: with a size up:

"Engine 71 on scene, several people are trapped on the upper levels. We are starting rescue operations. Fire appears to be on the back side of the apartment. Engine 72 you are primary attack."

I was still about 90 seconds out. Luckily the captain had the map open and was directing me in. As I rounded the corner toward the apartment, I could see the back side of the building was far off the road. My thoughts went to how much hose line I had for an initial attack. It wasn't enough, if I stayed on the road, so I did the only thing I could do: I sped up and jumped the curb, blowing through the snow. It was a lot of snow, but I got us about 20 yards closer. I was sure it would be close enough.

"Engine 72 on scene, making attack on rear side," we reported.

The captain and other firefighter baled for the hose line, while I went for the pump panel. I started priming the pump and getting ready to give them water. As I saw them reach the back door to the apartment, I charged the line. I knew these guys, and they will not stop until they get inside and get water on the fire, no matter how many floors they have to climb. With the amount of fire visible, I knew my crew was going to be flowing max water the entire time. That gave me about four minutes to connect to the fire hydrant, which was about 90 feet behind me. That feat would not be a big deal on dry, clear pavement, but I had 16 inches of snow and ice to pull the large heavy hose through. But I would do it, even if it killed me.

I rushed to the back of the engine and grabbed the hose line and started pulling. Each section of hose is 50 feet long and folded on in the bed of the engine at about every 15 feet. I dug in and was pulling as hard as I could, sections coming off. With each section, there was more weight and more friction. I was slipping and falling, getting up and pulling and falling, inching my way closer and closer to the hydrant. Through the falling snow, I saw figures emerging. It was the citizens of Noblesville, and I heard them say, "I will help." I was overjoyed and relieved! "We need to get to that hydrant," I told them. We reached the hydrant; I pulled the cap and connected the hose. Then I handed the hydrant wrench to one of them and told them to connect the other end to the engine. When I signaled, they were to crank the hydrant on.

By then a lot of time had passed and I knew my buddies were going to need that water. I made it to the engine, pulled the hose to the pump connection, and got it connected. I could barely see the hydrant and the guy standing there, but I raised my hands and waved. He saw me and started cranking the hydrant. I could see the water rushing to me as the hose sprang to life and filled with water. The engine pump surged with power as the water hit the impellers. "Thank God!" I thought. The main fire was knocked out within a couple of hours, then the next 20 hours or so were spent putting out small fires and doing investigations. Turns out it was an arson fire, and sadly, a pregnant mother and her young child perished in the fire.

Let me conclude by saying "thank you" to whoever those people were who voluntarily stepped up to help me with the hose. They made a difference that night on behalf of their neighbors and emergency responders.

YOUNG AND DUMB

by Steve

This story takes place when I was only about one year into my career with the fire department--about as fresh and green as they come. But I was all in for the important work of saving lives, and I cared deeply about doing my job well. One day the tones dropped for a run on a residential fire. I was the engine driver, with two others on our engine with me. We knew engine 72 was on the way, too. I was driving pedal to the metal and barreling through town, eager to save the home and anyone in it.

As we pulled up to the residence, we saw smoke billowing from the home. No information had been given on whether people were home or not when the fire began. My teammates pulled the fire hose from the bed of the truck, and when I saw them at the door, I charged the hose line, giving them all the water they needed. Then I left the truck and began a search. Inside, I first came to some stairs and went up them. The air was black with smoke, and I could only feel around for anything that seemed like a human body. On the floor, on top of a bed, under the bed, and then to the closet.

Suddenly, I felt a body laying in the closet! My heart was racing and I was praying as I grabbed the person under the arms and started dragging him down the stairs. I reached the front door and burst out with the person in my arms. I was out of breath and looked up to see firefighters and people just standing around. What is going on? I thought. Why are they not helping this victim? I pulled off my face mask and found them all laughing.

Then I heard my buddy say, "Dude, you just saved a mannequin!"

MAC-N-CHEESE

by Steve

Do you love Mac-N-Cheese, I SAID, DO YOU LOVE MAC-N-CHEESE! Me too and so do all the emergency responders. In fact, at the fire house, depending on how you made it, we could make an entire meal out of this mac-n-Cheese. Check it out.

Prep Time: **20 min.** | Cook Time: **50 min.** | Oven Temp: **350° F**

INGREDIENTS

- 16 oz. Macaroni
- 1 c. Parmesan Cheese, shredded
- 1 c. Swiss Cheese, shredded
- 1 c. White Cheddar Cheese, shredded
- 1 c. Gruyere Cheese, shredded
- ½ c. Onion, finely chopped
- 3 Tbsp. Black Pepper, ground
- 2 ½ c. Milk
- ¼ C Butter
- 1 lb. Bacon
- 3 Tbsp. Flour
- 1 lb. Beef or Chicken

INSTRUCTIONS

1. Mix all of the cheeses together.
2. Coat a 3-quart broiler-safe au gratin or baking dish with cooking spray; set aside.
3. Bring a large pot of lightly salted water to boiling.
4. Add pasta and cook according to package directions. 1b. Drain pasta, rinse and return to the warm pot. Set aside.
5. Preheat oven to 350°F
6. You have some choices to make here. What meats do you want to add. At the fire house the three main go to's were, Bacon, Chicken, Beef. You may want to add others, cool, do it.
7. Prepare your meats, cook them how ever you want but be sure they are crumbled or cut into small pieces.
8. In a saucepan melt the butter over medium heat.
9. Add onion; cook and stir for 3 minutes.
10. Stir in flour, and pepper.
11. Add milk all at once. Cook, whisking constantly, until thickened.
12. Pour in the cheese mixture and whisk until the entire mixture is blended together.
13. Mix the cheese mixture and the macaroni together.
14. Transfer mixture to prepared dish.
15. Bake for 45 minutes at 350 and then turn to broil for the last 5 minutes.

Steve's office was behind our dispatch center, He dressed as himself.....and so did I (Missy)

BREECH BIRTH

by Steve

It was about 3:00am when the tones for a run dropped at fire station 74, and I must have been in a REM sleep cycle because I vaguely remember sitting up on the side of the bed and being confused for a few seconds about where I was. But after 20 years as a firefighter, my head always cleared quickly, as it did then. I was the ladder engineer at that station, on duty that night with the lieutenant and the medic. As I headed for the engine, along with the other two, we heard dispatch announce the nature of the run:

"Engine 74, Ambulance 72, report of childbirth at (the caller's address)."

Childbirth at a residence is actually quite common and usually turns out not to be a serious issue. Often the mother is not even truly in labor and simply gets transported by ambulance WITH Basic Life Support (BLS). Anticipating probably another mild situation, we were, of course, prepared in case we encountered something worse.

All three of us were in the engine and running lights and sirens (Signal 10) to the scene in under 90 seconds, from a dead sleep. We arrived at the residence ahead of the ambulance, and the lieutenant marked us as on the scene.

"Dispatch, Ladder 74 arriving. There is a gentleman standing outside the residence."

Oh, good, I thought, this guy looks very calm. Everything must be alright. Probably just some false labor pains needing a transport BLS, if that.

We exited the engine, each grabbing our assigned supplies for this kind of run. When we asked the man what was happening, he very calmly replied, "My wife is in the kitchen, and she's in labor." Based on the man's demeanor I'm sure our medic was also thinking that this was probably not a serious situation. The house was well lit on the inside as we walked in and down a short hallway to an open-layout living room and kitchen.

Standing in the middle of the kitchen was an exceptionally calm but completely naked woman with the full leg of an unborn baby dangling out between her legs! We were utterly shocked! But it only took us a moment to spring into action like a well-oiled machine.

"Dispatch, advise expedite, this is a breech birth."

I sprinted to the engine, hearing the ambulance approaching. As I pulled the backboard and meds, the ambulance arrived, and I yelled back "We need the cot!" This was a serious situation, and even as highly trained and seasoned emergency responders, we were all sweating bullets and feeling a little panicked inside. But we maintained a professional demeanor. Amazingly, both the mother and father were calm, almost as if nothing was happening.. By the time I got back in the kitchen, the mother was receiving oxygen. After loading her on the backboard and then the cot, we began Advanced Life Support (ALS) transfer to the hospital.

On our way out to the ambulance, the lieutenant told the man that he could ride in the front of the ambulance. But the husband just told his wife, "Honey, I will just close up the house and see you there in a little while."

"Ok," she said. " Bring my bag when you leave!" I have never seen any two people so calm!

In the ambulance, the crew applied pressure to keep the infant in the birth canal while the medic administered IV's and arranged for arrival at the hospital. I followed in the ladder truck, running lights and sirens. When we arrived at the emergency room, two staff were waiting for us and whisked the mother away for an emergency C-section. Our team went to our designated staff office in the hospital to write our reports, which usually took about 60 to 90 minutes. We were wrapping up when one of the nurses from the ER came in and said, "It's a girl! Both mom and the baby are doing great." We were so glad that the situation turned out to be one of those rare times when we get both good news and closure.

DIRTY RICE AND SHRIMP

by Steve

This is a somewhat easy dish to prepare and each cook can add their own flare to the dish. I use brown rice and I like my rice on the al dente side for this dish but you can use any rice you like. The shrimp is where it gets a little weird. I chop up the shrimp into small chunks and it all gets mixed together. Crazy yes but as I watched Tom splash around in the fish tank and the chunks of shrimp falling through the water this is what I thought of. With my shrimp, I like it kind of spicy so this dish is prepared that way however, you can alter the amount of spicy-nest to your taste.

Prep Time: **15 min.** | Cook Time: **50 min.**

INGREDIENTS

12 oz Brown Rice

2 Tbsp. Granulated Beef Bouillon

1 Each Green and Red Pepper, Diced

1 clove Garlic

¼ tsp. Cayenne

½ tsp. Paprika

1 ½ tsp. Thyme

⅓ c. Green onion

3 Tbsp. Coconut Oil

3 Tbsp. Butter

Salt and Pepper to taste

2 lbs. Shrimp, Peeled and Deveined

INSTRUCTIONS

1. In a bowl combine the Coconut Oil & Butter, Green Onions, Peppers, Garlic, Salt and Pepper mix well.
2. Cook brown rice according to package directions in water along with the beef bouillon, cayenne, paprika and thyme.
3. When the rice is almost done cooking, heat a large heavy saucepan on medium-low heat.
4. Add the mixture and sauté on medium-low heat until soft and browned, about 12 minutes.
5. Add shrimp, cover and cook 5 more minutes.
6. When the shrimp is done, toss brown rice in with the shrimp, combine well and serve.

FISH TANK FEED

by Steve

Every morning after checking the fire engines and equipment, firefighters across the country will sit down for their coffee and have a social visit. On this particular morning, Dan, Tom, and I were the crew at my fire station. The three of us had worked together for a couple of years, and I would say we were good friends. A few stories down and Tom looks up, his head kind of tilted as if something just captured his attention, and says, "Fellas, I'm going to feed the fish." Now, Dan and I had already seen this little exercise unfold a few times, and we are already chuckling, so let me set the stage. Picture a 60-gallon freshwater tank with about 20 fish. This tank is positioned in what is basically a living room. There are four cloth-covered recliners, a TV, and a couple of end tables. The open area kitchen and table are next to this room, and that is where we are sitting.

Tom proceeds to the freezer and pulls out a small block of frozen shrimp, an item we purchased from the pet store the shift before. Walking to the tank, Tom raises the hinged wooden lid of the decorative tank cover with his left hand while at the same time submerging his right hand along with the shrimp block directly into the tank water. All the while talking to us: "Fellas, the only way to get these fish to eat is to break the shrimp up in the water; otherwise, the block sinks to the bottom." He is actually serious, and his hand is splashing all around in the water. "Look at them go! They are eating from my hand--just like my pups."

Knowing what's about to happen, I say, "Here, Tom, take some of these paper towels." But it's too late. Tom's wet hand and forearm exits the tank and in one seamless movement travels directly to the back of the cloth recliner where, in several stroking motions, he dries his arm. Astonished, we both yelled out about the paper towels, but Tom's response was classic Tom: "It's just a little water fellas. It'll dry up." Dan and I never sat in that recliner again.

FIRE HOUSE CHILI

by Steve

What fire house would be complete without a chili recipe on the menu? You can count on this; every fire fighter has their version of chili. Some are hot, other mild, and many are somewhere in between. Here is another thing you can count on, we firefighters all say our chili is the best. So here we go, try my chili. As always alter the spices to your liking. If you like it hot add that pepper, if you like it mild dial it back.

Prep Time: **10 min.** | Cook Time: **1 hr.**

INGREDIENTS

- 16 oz. Tomato Paste
- 64 oz. Tomato Juice
- 12 oz. Diced Tomatoes
- 1 lb. Ground Pork
- 1 lb. Ground Beef
- 16 oz. Chili Hot Beans
- 16 oz. Kidney Beans
- 16 oz. Back Beans
- 1 med-lg Onion, Chopped
- 2 Tbsp. Garlic
- 1 tsp. Habanero
- 1 tsp. Cayenne Powder
- 2 tsp. Cumin
- 2 tsp. Oregano
- 2 tsp. Parsley
- 1 lb. Elbow Macaroni

INSTRUCTIONS

1. Set macaroni aside.
2. Mix the meats together and place in a fry pan.
3. In a large kettle mix all other ingredients together.
4. Place kettle on medium and bring to a boil and then turn to simmer.
5. Brown the pork and beef in a large saute fry pan. Drain the meat, and add to sauce.
6. After 45 minutes bring a pot of water to boil and add macaroni. Cook to desired consistency and then drain rinse.
7. Add the cooked macaroni to the sauce.
8. Simmer for five minutes.

HE WALKS ON WATER

by Steve

Picture a hot summer mid-afternoon on a Saturday. It was just this kind of afternoon when I heard the tones drop at fire station 74 where I was a ladder engineer and the fire and rescue boat operator. The dispatch was for a sunken boat on nearby Morse Reservoir, with multiple people in the water. There were three of us on duty, but we knew others would be coming, too, from station 72. We rolled out in ladder 74 for the 60 second drive to the docks where rescue boat 74 was staged. It took 60 more seconds from the time we parked to launch it. We move kind of fast when there are lives to save! Boat 74 is a jet boat and can do about 35 knots, or 40 mph. We have lights and sirens, and there is a drop-down bow for rescues and for the dive team. It is equipped with a very accurate Lowrance sonar and depth finder. I knew the reservoir fairly well, so I knew it would take us about 90 seconds to reach the victims.

As we approached the incident location, we saw a very unusual sight. In front of us, about 100 yards from the shore, there was a man standing on top of the water! His feet were about 4 inches below the water line. In the water near him was another man, swimming around. The three of us on the boat scanned for others but did not see anyone else in the water. That could be a good thing, or we could possibly have to dive for someone submerged. I maneuvered the port side of the boat to the man in the water, and my crew mates helped him on board. He was fine and told us there was no one else in the water, except for the standing man. According to the Lowrance the water was 20 feet deep, so this man seemed to be performing a Jesus-like miracle!

I began maneuvering slowly toward the miracle man, with the indication on the Lowrance still showing 20 feet deep. We yelled to the man and asked him how he was floating on his feet in such deep water.

He yelled back, "I am not going to let my boat get away! I am standing on the bow!"

We could then see that he had the bow line in his hand, so we tied a buoy to the line and got him on board our boat. Engine 72 and ambulance 72 had arrived, and we notified dispatch to start a wrecker service. Ambulance 72 checked both men out on shore, and they signed a signature of release. When we asked the boat owner how this happened, he said that he was jumping wakes head on in his 1970 Chris Craft, just for fun, but he mistimed a particular wake and the bow of the boat went under the wake - essentially turning his boat into a submarine. The boat went under, and the bow, being lighter than the motor, flipped over toward the surface as the motor sunk.

The wrecker service soon arrived, and we started talking to the operators. Before we knew it, we looked up and the boat owner had pulled the cable from the back of the wrecker and jumped in the water. We rushed over and asked what the hell he was doing! He said he was going to swim the cable out to his boat and hook it up so they could pull it from the water.

"Look, sir, that cable is going to get very heavy trying to pull it 100 yards while swimming, plus we have a boat right here to do that! Go ahead and get out of the water," we told him.

We did allow him to ride out to his boat with us so that we could hook the line to the bow cleat. This turned out to be a bad decision on our part because even though we had him put on a life vest for the ride, as we approached the boat he ripped it off and dove overboard!

"What the hell are you doing?" we said again!

"Give me the line!" he told us. "I will hook it to my boat."

As they say, when you can't beat 'em, join 'em. So we let him hook up his precious boat to the wrecker, and we pulled it to shore, safe and sound.

CRISPY SKIN SALMON

by Steve

Call me crazy, but I could eat salmon for every meal. There are so many different ways to cook salmon and season salmon. Look, you are going to have to experiment with the seasoning. You almost can't go wrong as long as you don't overcook the salmon. You may want to try these. For a classic flavor, try adding garlic powder, dried basil, dried parsley, and onion powder. For a smokier taste, use paprika, chile powder, or cumin. For a lemony kick, dress with fresh lemon juice and lemon slices. chopped fresh rosemary, fresh parsley.

Prep Time: **10 min.** | *Cook Time:* **15 hrs.**

INGREDIENTS

- 4 8-oz. Center Cut Salmon Filets, 1 ¼ inch thick with skin on
- Salt and Pepper to taste
- 4 Tbsp. Oil, your choice – Coconut, Grape Seed or Olive
- 4 Tbsp. Butter, melted
- 4 wedges Lemon
- ¼ c. Panko Bread Crumbs
- ¼ c. Parmesan Cheese
- ½ c. Pistachios, finely crushed

INSTRUCTIONS

1. It is important to use a towel and pat dry the salmon
2. Lightly season salmon fillets with salt and pepper on both sides. If you love additional spices, do it.
3. Using a sharp knife, score the skin, this allows the heat to more evenly cook the salmon.
4. Combine 2 tablespoons butter, pistachios, panko bread crumbs, Parmesan cheese, in a small bowl; stir with a fork until combined
5. Pre-heat oven to 375 degrees
6. Coat an oven safe skillet with choice of oil, heat on medium high until it shimmers.
7. Place salmon fillets, skin-side down, sear for 2 minutes.
8. Add 2 tablespoons of butter to skillet, turn heat to low and begin basting the salmon, for 1 minute.
9. Top with pistachio mixture, pressing mixture down onto salmon.
10. Place skillet in oven and bake for 8 minutes or until salmon flakes easily. Fillets should be slightly pink in center.
11. Remove from oven, plate and serve with lemon wedges or sprinkle lemon juice.

CROQUE MONSIEUR PART 1 - BECHAMEL

by Steve

The Bechamel is what makes the Croque Monsieur, otherwise you just have a Ham and Cheese sandwich. This was a treat at the fire house, not only because it is so good, but because we would have a good time bantering back and forth about it being just a Ham and Cheese sandwich. I would argue, no it is a French Croque Monsieur. They would say, is it toasted bread, ham, cheese, and I would say for the most part, OK Ham and Cheese sandwich. Hilarious

Prep Time: **20 min.** | *Cook Time:* **10 min.**

INGREDIENTS

1 ½ c. Milk
½ c. Heavy Cream
3 Tbsp. Butter
3 Tbsp. All Purpose Flour
Pinch Ground Nutmeg
Salt and Black Pepper to taste

INSTRUCTIONS

1. Add milk and cream to a saucepan.
2. Add the butter to a saucepan. Have the flour ready, you are going to make a Roux.
3. Heat milk and cream mixture until hot not boiling.
4. Heat and melt butter on a medium low heat do not burn. When melted turn heat to low and begin adding the flour, stirring continuously for 3 minutes.
5. Pour in half the hot milk mixture stirring constantly. Once the milk is incorporated into the roux, add the remaining milk mixture and keep stirring.
6. Continue stirring on low until thicken, about a minute.
7. Remove from stove and set aside. The Béchamel Sauce will become thicker as it cools down. Note: this will be the spread for part two of making our Croque Monsieur.
8. Move to the Part two Croque Monsieur recipe.

CROQUE MONSIEUR PART 2 - SANDWICH

by Steve

Now the fun part, lets assemble the Croque Monsieur. There may seem like this requires a lot of steps, but it is mostly simple. At the firehouse I would act as if this was a complicated dish to make and we would all get a good laugh. Call it what you will, but this is a delicious sandwich.

Prep Time: **15 min.** | Cook Time: **8 min.**

INGREDIENTS

8 slices Ham, good quality
2 c. Gruyere Cheese
¾ c. Grated Parmesan Cheese
4 Tbsp. Butter

INSTRUCTIONS

1. Pick your bread. There are a verity of breads to choice from. A traditional Croque Monsieur will be made with Sweet Pain De Mie, but really you pick your favorite bread.
2. It is time to get your Bechamel on the counter top and get ready to use it. In other words, you are going to spread it on the bread.
3. Melt the butter on low and have a cooking brush ready to go. 4. Line a baking sheet with parchment paper.
4. Preheat the oven to 400 degrees.
5. Spread the melted butter on 1 side of each slice of bread.
6. Heat a large skillet over medium heat and brown the buttered side pieces of bread about 2 minutes. Place browned bread on the prepared baking sheet, browned side down.
7. Spread each piece of bread with Bechamel sauce, from edge to edge.
8. Place two slices of ham on the Bechamel and top with 1/2 cup of grated Gruyere cheese.
9. Place remaining bread grilled side up on top of each sandwich and spread the top with Bechamel.
10. Sprinkle the top of each sandwich with 2 tablespoon grated Gruyere cheese and 2 tablespoons grated Parmesan cheese.
11. Place the baking sheet in oven for 5 to 8 minutes or until golden brown on top.

Note: you may use the broiler in the last minute, but careful not to burn. Let's eat.

CHICKEN NOODLE SOUP

by Steve

Oh man, I add a lot of spice and richness to this chicken noodle soup. The guys at the firehouse love it that way. Ok, it's going to make you full and satisfied let's hope we don't catch a run for the next couple of hours. Yes, we all would say that about this meal. Wait who am I kidding, we would say that about almost every meal. It takes a lot of fuel to power us firefighters.

Prep Time: **30 min.** | Cook Time: **90 min.**

INGREDIENTS

- 2 lbs. Chicken Breasts
- 64 oz. Chicken Broth or Stock
- 4 c. Egg Noodles
- 2 Tbsp. Garlic (minced)
- 2 med. onions
- 6 stalks of celery
- 1 ½ lbs. carrots
- ¼ c. parsley
- ½ stick Butter
- Salt and Pepper to taste
- ⅓ Heavy Cream

INSTRUCTIONS

1. Cut the chicken into 1 to 2 inch cubes or streps. Alternatively you can shred the chicken after it is boiled.
2. Rinse and dry the chicken
3. Place the Chicken Broth or Stock in a large pot.
4. Chop the onions, celery, carrots, into small bit sized.
5. Let's start boiling the chicken in a pot of water. Bring to a full boil and then turn to low for 2 minutes.
6. Drain and rinse the chicken.
7. Place the chopped the onions, celery, carrots in the broth pot and bring to a rolling boil, then reduce to a very low boil and add the chicken.
8. Add the garlic, parsley, butter, salt and pepper and low boil for 45 minutes.
9. Increase the heat to a medium boil and add the noodles, cook for about 5 minutes.
10. Slowly add the cream while staring.
11. Turn the heat to low and allow to simmer for 5 minutes and serve.

Capes to Aprons • Stories and Recipes

FISH TANK SMACK DOWN

by Steve

Well here we are again at the fire station: a few buddies and me (see the "Dirty Rice and Shrimp" recipe for the context to this story). You know the drill: we have just finished the morning fire engine checks, and it's time for coffee and maybe a doughnut. There we are at the kitchen table, exchanging stories and catching up on each other's family drama. Then, like so many times before, Tom gets "the look." It goes something like this: Tom's head gives a slight twitch in the direction of whatever has caught his attention. In this case, it is once again that darn fish tank. As I told in the other fish tank story, Dan and I have seen this madness a few times already, or so we thought. As Tom gets up from the table and starts walking, we think he is heading for the freezer and the frozen shrimp to feed the fish. To our surprise, he walks straight to the tank.

"Tom," Dan says, "what are you doing, bud?"

Tom scratches the side of his chest and replies, "I think one of those fish plants is a little crooked."

"Tom," I reply, "it's not crooked. It's moving around with the current from the water pump."

"I don't know, fellas, I'm going to fix it."

Now let me describe the top hood of the tank. It is a solid wooden hood, rectangular in shape to fit over the tank. It looks very nice. The hood is hinged in the middle to allow the top front of the hood to swing open to add food or chemicals as needed. The entire hood can be removed for heavy cleaning or work inside the tank.

So Tom approaches the tank and grabs the hood on both ends. In a single lifting motion he raises the hood straight upward over his head while simultaneously rolling the back of the hood toward the ceiling and the front of the hood toward the floor. This allows the hinged lid of the hood to swing freely open, and this swinging motion hits Tom directly in the forehead with a loud thud! Dan and I burst into laughter as Tom explodes and begins cursing. As he recovers, he places the hood right back on top of the tank. He marches off cursing at us, as we cannot contain our laughter.

About ten minutes pass, and Tom finally comes back to the room. Without a single word, he approaches the tank again. And oh yes, Tom grabs the hood on both ends. In a single lifting motion, he lifts the hood straight upward over his head while simultaneously rolling the back of the hood toward the ceiling and the front of the hood toward the floor. The hinged lid swung open and hit Tom on the forehead with a thud - again! Dan and I burst into uncontrollable laughter - again. And Tom once again exploded into epic cursing. We did not see Tom the rest of the day. The next morning, everything was fine again, and the tank was left alone. Well, for awhile.

GRILLED PORK CHOP

by Steve

Mild flavor that can be sweet, exceptionally juicy and full of savory flavorful & succulent mild smoke flavor. Need I say more!

Prep Time: **8 min.** | *Cook Time:* **16 min.**

INGREDIENTS

- 6 1-inch Center Cut Loin Chops
- Olive Oil
- 1/8 c. Brown Sugar
- 1 tsp. Garlic Powder
- 1 tsp. Onion Powder
- ¾ tsp. Coarse Salt
- 1 tsp. Ground Black Pepper
- ½ tsp. Cayenne Pepper
- 2 Tbsp. Smoked Paprika

INSTRUCTIONS

1. Using small amounts of olive oil coat all chops. Then place them aside. Note: Wash and pat dry chops, before coating with the olive oil.
2. Add all ingredients together in a small bowl.
3. Break up clumps and fully combine all ingredients.
4. Now the important part, take your chops and hand apply the mixture to all sides, I mean really press it into the meat.
5. Head out to the grill.
6. Pre-heat grill to 450 to 500 degrees.
7. Seer the chops for about 2 to 3 minutes on each side. Note as you turn the chop place it on a different place on the grill, this way you get a clean hot surface.
8. After you have a nice seer on each side of the chops you can reduce the heat medium. Remember for pork you need a internal temperature of 150 degrees.
9. Use a meat thermometer or about five minutes for each 1/2-inch meat thickness.
10. Remove from grill and let rest about 2 minutes and Serve.

PEZ FINGER

by Steve

It was a slow day at the fire station, and a four-person euchre game was in full swing. Suddenly, the tones dropped for a run!

"Engine 71, Rescue 71, Medic 71, Ambulance 73, report of a traumatic hand injury. The caller is frantic and crying out uncontrollably. I am unable to gather additional info. Police are en route."

We had already sprung from our seats and raced to our apparatus. The rescue vehicle was first out the bay door, followed by the engine, where I was, and the medic directly behind. The location was a short drive from the station, so we arrived quickly. The ambulance and police were close behind us. As we grabbed medical gear for what we imagined was a horrific accident, we could hear the man crying and screaming from inside the residence. We rushed to the front door and made entry.

"Sir, it's ok, we are with the fire department and we are here to help!"

The young man emerged from the back of the house and approached us, still panicked and crying out while holding his left hand with his right hand. Kenny, our medic, reached him first and compassionately addressed him.

"Hey, buddy, what has happened?" he said.

The young man, still crying, held up his hand up and said, "I have this Pez Dispenser stuck on the end of my finger!"

Completely caught off guard, it took us all a few seconds to process just how ridiculous the situation was. I began laughing to myself, as I knew the others were, too, though we were careful to hide it.

"So this whole production is over a Pez candy dispenser?" our medic asked him in disbelief.

" Yes," the man replied, "it's stuck!"

The medic grabbed his affected hand then grabbed the Pez dispenser and with a slightly exaggerated but still gentle yank, he pulled the Pez off the man's finger. Voila, major trauma resolved!

PURPLE POTATO MASH

by Steve

I like to use purple potatoes but this recipe will work for almost any potato. I mean, it's mashed potatoes. Here's the thing, purple potatoes are supposed to be a little better for you. With foods we all have our own tastes so you can add slightly different amounts of spice and the other ingredients. I think the purple looks good on a plate. I mix my spices together and then taste the mixture. I will continue to adjust until I get it right

Prep Time: **15 min.** | *Cook Time:* **30 min..**

INGREDIENTS

2 lbs. Purple Potatoes

1 stick Butter, room temperature

½ - ¾ c. Half and Half

Salt to taste

½ tsp. Pepper

1 Tbsp. Chives, optional

1 tsp. Garlic, optional

Pinch Cayenne Pepper, optional

INSTRUCTIONS:

1. Wash and peel potatoes. Cut into slices.
2. Cut butter into slices.
3. Choose the spices you want and mix them together.
4. Place half and half in a metal pot.
5. Place potatoes in pot with water about an inch over the potatoes.
6. Bring the water to a boil for about 3 minutes then reduce to a low boil until a fork can easily go through the potatoes, about 15 minutes.
7. Place the half and half on a burner and set to low, keep an eye on this so not to burn half and half.
8. When potatoes are ready drain the water, rinse quickly and place potatoes in mixer.
9. Add warm half and half.
10. Begin mixing, when mixed together add the spice mixture.
11. Continue mixing until at your desired consistency.

Usually this is a side dish so make sure you are ready before you prepare your potatoes. They will not stay hot for long.

WHAT'S THAT SMELL?

by Steve

We all know the feeling of "déjà vu" - the sense that something has happened before or is strangely familiar. Often I just can't place it or it is so out of context that I can't make the connection, so I just brush it off. But sometimes, it clicks. One of the most common déjà vu experiences people have is with smell. This has happened to me several times in my life, including one particular instance that occurred early in my career at the fire department. I was a back stepper on Engine 71, which was located at headquarters - the old headquarters, which was a two-story brick building. I remember it was early summer. On this particular day, around 6:00 p.m., the crew had just finished dinner. There were four of us on duty: the captain, the engineer, and two back steppers. We were sitting downstairs in the bay just talking and telling stories. Suddenly, the fire phone signaled its alarm (yes, the emergency calls came directly to a red telephone in the bay). It was loud and had a distinct sound so that we would know it was an emergency call. Every time this phone alarmed it startled the daylights out of me, probably because I was so new.

The captain immediately answered the phone while the rest of us made our way to our fire gear, in case it was a real emergency.

"Noblesville Fire, do you have an emergency?" said the captain.

On the other end of the line were the yells of a person in real distress: "My house is on fire! It's on fire!"

We could vaguely hear the caller. The captain raised his hand and did a finger spin in the air; this was the hand sign to roll. We kicked it into high gear, donning fire gear and moving to the engine, all while the captain was trying to get the information we needed to respond.

"What is the address? Where is the fire located? Is everyone out?" he asked the caller. "Stay out and keep everybody back. We are on our way!"

The engine was already running when he finished. The other back stepper and I are in the back of the cab putting our SCBA and facemasks on. We were ready to do battle with this fire dragon! In just over one minute since the telephone rang, the captain was in the engine with the address, and we were off. Out the bay door we went, lights flashing, sirens blaring, air horn sounding! The two of us in the back were amped up. We knew we needed to pull the fire hose and make an entry when we arrived; the only thing we didn't know was where the captain would tell us to start that entry.

A sharp left turn, and as we feel the engine decelerate, we hear the size-up from the captain: "Engine 71 on the scene of a single story working residence, smoke is rolling, smoke is rolling from the roof. We will be offensive through the front."

As the engine came to a complete stop, we two back steppers were already off and grabbing the inch and a half hose line from the bed of the engine. As we passed the captain, he told us to make our entry through the front. It was up to the two of us, since the other engines on their way had not arrived yet, the engineer had to stay with the engine to make sure we had water, and the captain had to direct the entire evolving scene or complete chaos could unravel. As we reached the front entry, we paused for just a second as the engineer charged the hose, and we opened the nozzle slightly so that the rushing water could force air from the line. Whoosh, the water started flowing! We controlled the flow and burst into the front of the house, staying low. All we saw was dense smoke as we worked our way back, searching for the source of the fire. We were also looking for victims along the way.

As we reach the back of the house, what we thought was probably a bedroom, we saw the dragon fire, bright red and orange, flickering and dancing before us, as if to say, "You are mine!" But not today! We had trained for this, and as we spotted the seat of the fire dragon, we unleashed 250 pounds per square inch of quenching water. The hose pushed back on us as we drove forward in a sweeping motion, forcing our way closer and closer to this monster. The fire dragon lashed back - cracking, charging, billowing smoke in our direction, trying to drive us back. But we were relentless. We knew how to work the water to our advantage, changing the direction of the hose stream and spray pattern. Finally, we killed the dragon!

By then, about 10 minutes had passed, and we knew we did not do this by ourselves. The other engines had arrived, and they were taking action on the outside - cutting openings for ventilation, letting the smoke out, and turning off electrical power to the residence. With the fire under control, we make our way out to get new orders. Outside we saw a bustle of activity. As I removed my SCBA, I smelled an unusual odor - a little like a normal house fire but with an additional strange yet vaguely familiar smell that I just couldn't place. It was déjà vu for sure!

"You two change out your bottles and get back in there to start an overhaul and tell us if you see anything unusual," the captain ordered.

This directive was great for me because I was young and gung-ho and wanted to go back inside. As my partner and I were changing SCBA bottles, my déjà vu connection finally came to me!

I looked at my partner, who had a huge smile, and I said, "Bud, this is a grow house!"

"Oh yes it is!" he replied, and we burst into laughter.

The whole neighborhood smelled like marijuana, and once the smoke from the burning house started to clear, the smell got stronger.

"Hey," I told my partner, "the reason that dragon was dancing around us like that was because she was higher than a kite!"

Back inside, we went directly to the room of the fire. Sure enough, there were the charred remains of containers with dirt and what looked like light fixtures. We radioed the captain and told him there was confirmation of growing paraphernalia. When we went to the adjoining room, the grow operation was even more obvious, since that room was largely unburned, with only some smoke damage. There were plants and plenty of grow lights. We again radioed our findings to the captain. As he responded back to us that he had received our information, we could hear multiple people snickering in the background. Plenty of laughter was shared that day!

MAN ON THE RUN

by Steve

When I was part of the Hamilton County Emergency Management Search and Rescue team, our UAVs (unmanned aerial vehicles) came to the rescue one bitter cold December night for an important mission. The temperatures were in the low twenties, and the wind was even colder. There were several inches of snow on the ground, and light to moderate snow was falling. It was only a few days before Christmas, but someone who clearly did not have the Christmas spirit robbed a gas station at gunpoint. Thankfully no one was injured, but it turned into a police chase involving Hamilton County sheriff deputies and Boone County police agencies. The situation was dangerous on many levels: the armed suspect, the ice and snow-covered roads, and the bitter cold. We knew it could be a rough chase.

After about 20 minutes, the suspect crashed his car about a mile or so across the county line in a rural area and then fled on foot. As the suspect faded from view, running into the tree line, officers requested the Hamilton County Emergency Management Search and Support Drone Team. I made up one half of this team, and we immediately responded, as we always do, with lights and sirens. The road conditions were passable but deteriorating. We arrived within 30 minutes and received our briefing and instructions. A perimeter had been established approximately one mile south of where the suspect had bailed. The area consisted of hundreds of acres of fields with a patchwork of wooded areas and several farmhouses and barns. The police tactical team had arrived and were going to start searching all of the farms in the direction where the suspect was believed to be heading. Our assignment was to move to a road at the south perimeter and begin airborne drone searches north toward the tactical team and report any findings.

We decided, given the conditions, that it was better to stay together and operate only one drone at a time. We had no LEO (law enforcement officer) with us, so while one of us was flying, the other could watch the ground for the suspect. The last thing we would want is to be looking up at the drone and have someone walk up on us! Another reason was that this was going to be a challenging flight, requiring lots of batteries, so if one drone failed, we could get the other drone up. So we got the drone airborne and began using Forward-Looking Infrared (FLIR) so we could see all of the hot spots. We also had a pair of FLIR binoculars so we could see what was going on around us.

At first we only targeted a few deer, maybe a coyote, and a couple of rabbits, but no suspect yet. After a couple of flights, we heard the police say that they have tracks and a possible suspect in a barn. They were going "live tactical," meaning live gunfire if needed. We positioned the drone near the site, and we could see the barn and the police approaching. It was at that moment that both my partner and I realized we were directly down range from the target site - potentially in the line of fire! We both immediately moved to the opposite side of the truck near the wheel rims, hoping for some level of protection but knowing nonetheless that the high-powered rifle bullets would easily pass clean through. We brought the drone back so that we could make a quick exit to the east, away from the line of fire. As we drove away, we could hear the tactical team on the radio saying, "Breach! Breach! Breach!" - meaning they made entry. A minute or so later, we heard them say, "Stand down, all clear." The suspect had been there but was gone.

A few more minutes passed when I heard a popping sound - pop! pop! - and a voice over the radio saying, " Shots fired! Shots fired! No location known. Units go tactical." Another few minutes of police chatter on the radio and an officer reported, "Stand down. Shooter located. It's a hunter, and he has been advised to secure his firearms and leave the area." Apparently even with 30 police cars, lights, and sirens in the area, this hunter still thought it was a good time to go hunting.

My partner and I relocated one mile east of our original location and got the drone airborne again, looking for any signs of a person on foot. At least two hours had passed by that point, which was a long time for someone to still be outside exposed to the elements on such a cold night. I was starting to think that this incident would likely be discontinued and the police would have to locate the suspect by other means. Then over the radio came the confident voice of the dispatcher: "All units be advised, the possible suspect has been seen moving through a field three miles south of your location and approximately one mile west of I-65." That news was the boost we all needed!

As we landed the drone to change locations, police car after police car passed us en route to the new site. We quickly got underway, too, working our way to I-65 in the southbound lane. We were quite a distance now from where we started the search. The weather had continued to deteriorate, and we were limited on how high and how long we could stay in the air. I was working the radio, and my partner was flying the drone. We searched on the west side of the interstate, moving south. Just under half a mile from our take-off location, the FLIR picked up a large thermal contact in the ditch on the west side. It was difficult to tell what it was, but we began investigating. All of a sudden, the contact leapt to the east across the interstate. That had to be the suspect!

I began making alert notifications on the radio and providing suspect location information. But we were on a Boone County channel, so I wasn't sure if everyone was getting the information who needed to know. I switched to my phone and called directly to the officer in charge.

"Lieutenant, the drone has the target suspect in sight," I reported.

I conveyed all of the location information via phone, which was not ideal but it worked nevertheless, and that was the important thing. My partner and I could see the suspect move into a neighborhood and begin going from house to house. We presumed he was probably trying to find shelter. I continued providing directions to the police until we saw several of them arrive and begin approaching the suspect's location with rifles raised. Then, in beautiful thermal imaging, we saw the suspect walk toward the police with hands up and fall to the ground as the police secured him. He had traveled almost 6 miles from where he bailed from his car, and he was so frostbitten that he put up no resistance.

We found out later that he never even heard the drone as we tracked him.

Steve with Grand Baby and his Ladder Truck

From Capes to Aprons
911 Emergency Dispatchers and Their Amazing Stories

You may never see them, you may never know they are next to you, but these unsung heroes are all about you. They are the dispatchers, police officers, firefighters, military, medical professionals, teachers, service workers, and many more. Most of us will never need their help, but rest assured they will be there if we do. They sometimes make great sacrifices to meet the needs of people they will never even know. They work countless hours of overtime and fill in to ensure there is never a gap in service to the community. Most centers have an "on-call" system which means if someone calls in sick, the "on-call" person has to be available to work. Imagine having that life and having to be available on your days off "just in case." They are cursed at, faulted, criticized, demeaned, belittled, hardly ever praised, but yet you still call upon them to rescue you in your time of need. They always answer the call, provide reason and compassion, and get you the help you desperately need……always.

~Missy Birnell Haston~

Many of the Dispatchers featured in this book remember Opening Day at the new Hamilton County Dispatch Center in Noblesville, IN in January, 2012. Although they are still located in this space, they continue to update service in order to serve the community as efficiently as possible.

www.ingramcontent.com/pod-product-compliance
Lightning Source LLC
Chambersburg PA
CBHW080747060526
44119CB00072B/179